DSA®
DRIVING STANDARDS AGENCY
SAFE DRIVING FOR LIFE

D0346082

the **official DSA** guide to
LEARNING
TO RIDE

21

Approved by
Plain
English
Campaign

London: TSO

Written and compiled by Driving Standards Agency (DSA) Learning Materials.

Published with the permission of the Driving Standards Agency on behalf of the Controller of Her Majesty's Stationery Office.

Previously known as *Official Motorcycling – CBT, theory & practical test*
First published 1998
Fourth edition 2003

New title - *The Official DSA Guide to Learning to Ride*
Fifth edition 2005
Third impression 2007

ISBN 978 011 552645 5

A CIP catalogue record for this book is available from the British Library.

Other titles in the official DSA series

The Official DSA Theory Test for Car Drivers
The Official DSA Theory Test for Motorcyclists
The Official DSA Theory Test for Drivers of Large Vehicles
The Official DSA Guide to Learning to Drive
Helping Learners to Practise - the official DSA guide
The Official DSA Guide to Driving - the essential skills
The Official DSA Guide to Riding - the essential skills
The Official DSA Guide to Driving Buses and Coaches
The Official DSA Guide to Driving Goods Vehicles
The Official DSA Guide to Tractor and Specialist Vehicle Driving Tests
The Official DSA Theory Test for Car Drivers (CD-Rom)
The Official DSA Theory Test for Motorcyclists (CD-Rom)
The Official DSA Guide to Hazard Perception (DVD) (also available on VHS)
Prepare for your Practical Driving Test (DVD)

Directgov

Directgov is the place to find all government motoring information and services. From logbooks to licensing, from driving tests to road tax, go to:

www.direct.gov.uk/motoring

Theory and practical tests
(Bookings and enquiries)

Online **www.direct.gov.uk/drivingtest**
DSA **0870 0101 372**
Fax **0870 0104 372**
Minicom **0870 0106 372**
Welsh speakers **0870 0100 372**

DVA (Northern Ireland)
Theory test **0845 600 6700**
Practical test **0870 247 2471**

Driving Standards Agency
(Headquarters)

www.dsa.gov.uk

Stanley House, 56 Talbot Street, Nottingham NG1 5GU

Tel **0115 901 2500**
Fax **0115 901 2510**

Driver & Vehicle Agency (Testing) in Northern Ireland

www.dvani.gov.uk

Balmoral Road, Belfast BT12 6QL

Tel **02890 681 831**
Fax **02890 665 520**

Driver & Vehicle Licensing Agency
(GB licence enquiries)

www.dvla.gov.uk

Longview Road, Swansea SA6 7JL

Tel **0870 240 0009**
Fax **01792 783 071**
Minicom **01792 782 787**

Driver & Vehicle Agency (Licensing) in Northern Ireland

www.dvani.gov.uk

County Hall, Castlerock Road, Coleraine BT51 3TB

Tel **02870 341 469**
24 hour tel **0345 111 222**
Minicom **02870 341 380**

Office of the Parliamentary Commissioner for Administration

(The Parliamentary Ombudsman)

Millbank Tower, Millbank, London SW1P 4QP

Tel **020 7217 4163**
Fax **020 7217 4160**

The Driving Standards Agency (DSA) is an executive agency of the Department for Transport. You'll see its logo at theory and practical test centres.

DSA aims to promote road safety through the advancement of driving standards, by

- establishing and developing high standards and best practice in driving and riding on the road; before people start to drive, as they learn, and after they pass their test
- ensuring high standards of instruction for different types of driver and rider
- conducting the statutory theory and practical tests efficiently, fairly and consistently across the country
- providing a centre of excellence for driver training and driving standards
- developing a range of publications and other publicity material designed to promote safe driving for life.

The Driving Standards Agency recognises and values its customers. We will treat all our customers with respect, and deliver our services in an objective, polite and fair way.

The Driver & Vehicle Agency (DVA) is an executive agency within the Department of the Environment for Northern Ireland.

Its primary aim is to promote and improve road safety through the advancement of driving standards and implementation of the Government's policies for improving the mechanical standards of vehicles.

www.dvani.gov.uk

www.dsa.gov.uk

Contents

section **one**
GETTING STARTED

This section covers

- About this book
- What is CBT?
- The CBT course
- Approved Training Bodies
- Your motorcycle licence

Message from the Chief Driving Examiner

Over the years various pieces of legislation have been introduced to reduce moped and motorcycle rider casualties, including the compulsory wearing of safety helmets, restrictions on the size of motorcycle a learner can ride and the requirement for all learner riders to pass a theory test.

Compulsory Basic Training (CBT) was introduced in 1990 to equip new riders with basic skills before riding unaccompanied on the road. CBT isn't a test and there's no exam – it's a course of training you're required to complete satisfactorily. As a road safety initiative it has proved to be a great success and motorcycling today is safer than it has ever been.

On the other hand, the purpose of the practical test is to prove that you can ride your motorcycle safely on the road. During your practical test your examiner will want to see you riding to the standards set in this book.

Those riding standards are given here in an easy-to-read style with illustrations which explain simply what is required.

However, riding is never predictable. Road conditions or circumstances will demand that you use your initiative or common sense. You should be able to assess any situation and apply the guidance given in this book.

You shouldn't assume that if you pass your tests you're a good rider with nothing more to learn. Learning to ride a motorcycle is a continuous process, and the tests are just one stage in your riding career.

Make sure that your aim is always 'Safe riding for life'.

Trevor Wedge

Trevor Wedge
Chief Driving Examiner and Director of Safer Driving

About this book

This book is designed to help you get the most out of the CBT course. Refer to it as you progress through each element and it will help you gain a better understanding of what you need to achieve. The useful advice will help you learn to ride competently and prepare for and pass your practical motorcycle test.

Important factors

You're just beginning your motorcycling career and this book is only one of the important factors in your training. Other factors you need to consider include

- finding a good instructor
- adopting a positive attitude
- patience and practice.

How you choose to develop as a motorcyclist is up to you. You should aim to be a safe and confident rider for life. Don't just put on a show for your test and then revert to a lower standard. Take pride in always setting a good example.

CBT will give you the basic skills you need to begin riding safely on the road

How will each part of this book help me?

Section one - Outlines the five elements of the CBT course and tells you what you need to know about your motorcycle licence.

Section two - Explains the details of each element of the CBT course.

Section three - Contains advice on how to continue your training after CBT and tells you what you need to do before the test.

Section four - Details the motorcycle test requirements and gives simple, clear advice. Refer to it regularly when preparing for your test.

Section five - Gives details about the extended test for disqualified riders.

Section six - Gives other useful information including addresses which may be helpful. There is also a personal CBT training record which you can use to keep track of your progress through your CBT course.

Books to help you study

The official DSA range will provide you with a sound knowledge of riding skills and safe riding practices.

The Official DSA Theory Test for Motorcyclists - Contains all the official theory test questions for motorcyclists including thorough explanations of the answers.

The Official DSA Guide to Riding - the essential skills - This is the official reference book, giving practical advice and best practice for all riders.

The Highway Code - Essential reading for all road users. It contains the most up-to-date advice on road safety and the laws which apply to all road users.

Know Your Traffic Signs - This contains most of the signs and road markings that you are likely to come across.

The information in these books will be relevant throughout your riding life so make sure you always have an up-to-date copy that you can refer to.

Other media

The Official DSA Theory Test for Motorcyclists (CD-Rom) - This provides an interactive way of learning. You can also practise taking a mock theory test.

The Official Guide to Hazard Perception (DVD) - An interactive DVD designed to help you prepare for the hazard perception parts of the theory and practical tests. It has clear guidance on how to recognise and respond to hazards and is packed with useful tips, quizzes and expert advice. It also includes official hazard perception video clips with feedback on your performance.

Alternatively, there is a video and booklet pack available.

These training materials are available online at **www.tsoshop.co.uk/dsa** or by mail order from **0870 241 4523**.

They are also available from all good bookshops and other outlets.

What is CBT?

It is the course which all learner motorcycle and moped riders must complete before riding on the road.

In addition, holders of a full car licence obtained by passing their driving test on or after 1 February 2001 must complete a CBT course if they wish to validate the full moped entitlement on their driving licence.

CBT can only be given by Approved Training Bodies (ATBs) who have instructors that have been assessed by DSA and sites approved by DSA for off-road training.

CBT allows you to learn the following in a safe environment

• motorcycling theory
• skills which make you safe on the road
• the correct attitude towards motorcycling.

Exemption from CBT

You don't have to take CBT if you hold a

• full moped licence obtained by passing a moped test after 1 December 1990
• full motorcycle licence for one category and wish to upgrade to another.

You will also be exempt if you live and ride on specified offshore islands. However, if you ride across to mainland UK you will need to complete a CBT.

Certificate of Completion

When you complete a CBT course you'll be given a Certificate of Completion of an Approved Training Course (DL196).

From 1 February 2001 the DL196 will record whether CBT was completed on

• a moped or motorcycle
• a motorcycle-sidecar combination or moped that has more than two wheels.

This will validate your entitlement accordingly.

Certificate life - CBT certificates have a two-year life.

A certificate validating full moped entitlement on a full car licence will remain valid for mopeds, for the life of the licence.

Motorcycle validation - If training is completed on a motorcycle-sidecar combination or on a moped that has more than two wheels

• moped validation will be limited to mopeds with more than two wheels
• motorcycle validation will be limited to motorcycle-sidecar combinations.

The CBT course

CBT is arranged so that you progress through a series of elements. You will only move onto the next element when your instructor is satisfied you have learnt the necessary theory and demonstrated the practical skills to a safe basic level.

Within each element the instructor is free to deliver the training in the order which is felt to be most appropriate for you.

The CBT record in part six of this book will allow you to record when each of the elements has been completed.

What are the elements?

Element A - Introduction

Element B - Practical on-site training

Element C - Practical on-site riding

Element D - Practical on-road training

Element E - Practical on-road riding

The elements must be taken in this order. Each element is described in detail in section two (see p18).

Instructor to trainee ratios

During your CBT you may be accompanied by other learners up to a maximum ratio of

- 4:1 during on-site elements
- 2:1 during the on-road element.

For those using the Direct Access scheme (see p16) the ratios are 2:1 for both on-road and off-road elements.

Your instructor will ensure you complete each element before you progress to the next

Approved Training Bodies

Types of instructor

CBT can only be given by ATBs using instructors who are either

- DSA assessed certified instructors or
- Down-trained certified instructors.

DSA Assessed Certified Instructors - Every ATB must employ at least one instructor who has successfully attended DSA's CBT assessment. They're called Cardington Assessed Instructors and can

- provide CBT training and issue DL196 certificates
- down-train other instructors within the ATB.

Down-trained Certified Instructors - These instructors have been down-trained by the Cardington Assessed Instructor and are qualified to provide CBT training including issuing the DL196 certificate at the end of the course.

Direct Access - Some instructors may have a further qualification allowing them to give Direct Access instruction. This is obtained by attending DSA's Direct Access Scheme assessment.

How can I tell which type of instructor is giving me training? - When training, your instructor will be carrying a certificate. If it contains a 'C' they are a Cardington Assessed Instructor while a 'D' indicates they are Direct Access qualified. Some certificates contain both qualifications.

Quality control

DSA monitors the standard of training given by instructors. If a DSA examiner is present during your training, don't worry. The examiner will not take part in the training; they are only there to safeguard the quality of training you receive.

Choosing an ATB

You can find out about the ATBs in your area from

- the local road safety officer
- most motorcycle dealers
- motorcycle papers and magazines
- local papers or Yellow Pages
- calling DSA on 0115 901 2500
- going online.

Clothing

Your instructor will discuss motorcycle clothing in detail as part of the CBT course.

If you are just starting to ride it will pay you to listen to your instructor before rushing out to buy anything.

During your CBT course you

- must wear the visibility aid provided by the ATB. This will carry the name of the training organisation
- should wear appropriate clothing and stout footwear.

Many ATBs provide basic equipment for the CBT course (See Element A p18).

Use your trainer's experience to make sure you get the best clothing you can for your money

Hiring a motorcycle

ATBs usually have motorcycles you can hire for your CBT, practical test or additional training.

These may be learner-rated motorcycles or Direct Access-rated motorcycles. Talk to local ATBs to find out what they can offer.

If you hire equipment and the machine from the ATB, they should provide the necessary insurance.

Your motorcycle licence

To begin riding a motorcycle on the road you must

- be at least 17 years old
- hold a valid DL196 certificate
- hold a driving licence which allows you to ride motorcycles (Category A).

That licence can be any of the following

- a provisional driving licence. This provides provisional car, motorcycle and moped entitlement
- a full car or moped licence. This provides provisional motorcycle entitlement.

All riders must wear a safety helmet at all times when riding, (unless they are a member of the Sikh religion and wear a turban) and ensure any helmet visor used conforms to BSI standards (see p20).

Provisional motorcycle entitlement

After completing CBT learners may ride a solo motorcycle up to 125 cc or with a power output of no more than 11 kW.

Learners who wish to ride a sidecar outfit can do so as long as it has a power-to-weight ratio not exceeding 0.16 kW/kg.

With provisional motorcycle entitlement you must not

- ride on motorways
- carry a pillion passenger
- ride without L plates fitted to both front and rear of the motorcycle (in Wales you may display red D plates). If you cross from Wales into another part of the UK you must display L plates.

Does a non-UK driving licence entitle me to ride?

You can ride for one year from the date of entry to the UK if you hold a valid foreign licence, after this you may be required to take a test depending on the country of origin of your licence. For further information please contact the DVLA (see details on p3).

Do I need to request motorcycle entitlement to be added?

Since March 2002 provisional motorcycle entitlement has automatically been included on driving licences. If you hold a provisional licence where the motorcycle entitlement has expired you'll need to contact DVLA for a replacement licence.

Full motorcycle licence

There are two types of full motorcycle licence, Sub-category A1 and Category A. A full motorcycle licence allows you to ride without L plates (or D plates in Wales), carry a pillion passenger and use motorways.

Sub-category A1 (light motorcycle licence) - A full A1 licence allows you to ride machines up to 125 cc and with a power output of up to 11 kW (14.6 bhp).

You can obtain a full sub-category A1 licence by passing the practical test on a bike of more than 75 cc but less than 125 cc.

Category A - A full category A licence gives you full entitlement to all machines.

You can obtain a full category A licence with a two-year qualifying period or without a two-year qualifying period via Direct Access.

Category A with two-year qualifying period - This will be obtained by passing the motorcycle test on a motorcycle of between 121 cc and 125 cc and capable of at least 100 km/h (62.5 mph).

Riders who are subject to the two-year qualifying period will be restricted to machines of 25 kW (33 bhp) maximum, and power-to-weight ratio not exceeding 0.16 kW/kg, for two years from the date of passing their test. At the end of that time any size of motorcycle may be ridden without taking another test.

While learning to ride red L plates must be fitted to the front and rear of your motorcycle

Category A via Direct Access - This is for riders aged 21 or over. Passing the motorcycle test on a machine of at least 35 kW (46.6 bhp) gives immediate access to all sizes of motorcycle.

You can practise on any size of motorcycle which exceeds the UK learner specification provided that

- you are accompanied at all times by a qualified approved instructor, on another motorcycle and in radio contact
- fluorescent or reflective safety clothing is worn during supervision
- L plates (D plates in Wales) are fitted and provisional licence restrictions followed.

Accelerated Access - This option is for riders who are subject to the two-year qualifying period and are at least 21 years old before this qualifying period is complete.

You can take a further test to give you immediate access to all motorcycles. This test must be taken on a motorcycle with a power output of at least 35 kW (46.6 bhp).

You can practise for this test on motorcycles above 25 kW (33 bhp) provided

- you're accompanied at all times by an approved instructor, on another motorcycle and in radio contact
- fluorescent or reflective safety clothing is worn during supervision
- L plates (or D plates in Wales) are fitted and provisional licence restrictions followed.

Good preparation is the key to the theory test (see page 9 for details of official revision aids)

Will I have to take a theory test?

All candidates for a practical test must first pass a motorcycle theory test, unless

- upgrading from A1 to A, or upgrading an A under the Accelerated Access scheme
- a full moped licence is held which was obtained by passing the moped test after 1 July 1996.

How do you define a moped?

A moped has an engine under 50 cc and doesn't weigh more than 250 kg. If it was registered before 1 August 1977 the moped can be moved by pedals

After 1 August 1977, it must have a maximum design speed not exceeding 50 km/h (31 mph).

Moped riders

To ride a moped on the road you must be at least 16 years old and have a driving licence that entitles you to ride mopeds (Category P). At 16 years old this can be a full or provisional moped licence.

For 17 and over it can also be a

- full car licence (see right)
- full motorcycle licence
- provisional driving licence. This provides provisional moped entitlement.

Mopeds are not allowed on motorways, even if you hold a full licence.

Remember, the same DL196 that validates your full moped entitlement will have a limited life (see Certificate life) for validating provisional motorcycle entitlement.

Provisional moped entitlement - After completing CBT this allows you to ride a moped. You must not carry a pillion passenger, ride on motorways or ride without red L plates (or D plates in Wales) fitted to both the front and the rear.

Full moped licence - Full moped entitlement allows you to ride mopeds without L plates and carry a pillion passenger.

Full car licence holders

Holders of a full car licence obtained by passing their driving test before 1 February 2001 hold unconditional full moped entitlement.

Holders of a full car licence obtained by passing their driving test on or after 1 February 2001, who do not already hold a full moped or motorcycle licence, must hold a valid DL196 to validate their full moped entitlement.

If a valid DL196 is already held when the car test is passed, the full moped entitlement will be validated immediately.

A DL196 validating full moped entitlement on a full car licence will remain valid for mopeds, for the life of the licence. It is therefore particularly important that the DL196 is kept safe.

Element A
Introduction to CBT

This element is an introduction to CBT. It will take the form of a discussion. Your instructor will explain the basics and not get involved in complicated issues.

Wherever possible your instructor will use examples to help demonstrate the point being made.

As a part of this element you'll have your entitlement to ride motorcycles checked.

If necessary your instructor will explain what you need to do in order to obtain this entitlement.

At the end of this module you should understand the purpose and content of CBT. Many experienced car drivers who take up motorcycling find that CBT is an eye opening experience which increases their awareness of hazards.

Your instructor will progress through the course at a pace that suits you. Don't be afraid to ask if you have not understood something

CBT overview

You cannot ride on the road until you have satisfactorily completed all the elements of CBT. Your instructor will explain the aims of CBT and will also explain why it was introduced. An overview of the course content should be given.

Remember, don't treat CBT as a formality you must grudgingly endure. Instructors are experienced motorcyclists who have valuable advice to give learner riders and are motorcycle enthusiasts.

Take the CBT course seriously and enjoy learning safely.

The time it takes to complete the course will be determined by you. Your instructor should not move you on to the next part until you're ready.

Within each element instructors are free to deliver the topics in the order that they find best for you. Every topic must, however, be covered to the necessary level.

You'll need to demonstrate to your instructor that you have a basic skill level and an understanding of each topic. This may be through question and answer sessions for the theory or through practical demonstrations of your riding ability.

Equipment and clothing

Your instructor will explain the different types of motorcycle clothing available. As well as looking at outer clothing, the talk will include helmets, visors and goggles, gloves and boots.

Motorcycle equipment is generally expensive and your instructor will help prioritise which equipment you should buy first and identify less expensive alternatives. You should also discuss the effects of getting cold and wet and how some clothing can help protect from certain injuries.

As well as being a good fit, your helmet must be correctly fastened

Safety helmets - By law, you must wear a safety helmet when riding a motorcycle on the road (members of the Sikh religion who wear a turban are exempt). All helmets sold in the UK must either comply with British Standard BS 6658:1985 and carry the BSI kitemark or

- comply with UNECE Regulation 22.05 (it will be marked with a UN 'E' mark - the first two digits of the approval number will be '05')

- comply with any standard accepted by a member of the European Economic Area (EEA) State which offers a level of safety and protection equivalent to BS 6658:1985 and carry a mark equivalent to the BSI kitemark.

Visors and goggles - A visor or goggles are vital to protect your eyes from wind, rain, insects and road dirt.

All visors and goggles must

- comply with British Standard BS 4110 Grade X, XA, YA or ZA
- display a BSI kitemark or
- comply with a European standard which offers a level of safety and protection at least equivalent to these British Standards and carry a mark equivalent to the BSI kitemark (ECE 22-05).

Goggles may comply with the EU Directive on Personal Protective Equipment and carry the 'CE' mark.

Eyesight check

At this stage in CBT your instructor will check your eyesight. The regulations state that, in good daylight, you should be able to read a vehicle number plate with letters 79.4 mm (3.1 inches) high at a minimum distance of 20.5 metres (about 67 feet). These are normally the number plates in the older format (for example X123XXX).

Number plates in the format (XX50XXX) have a narrower font and should be read from a distance of 20 metres (66 feet).

Your instructor will check your eyesight by asking you to read a number plate from a set distance

What if I can't read the number plate?

If you can't read the number plate at the minimum distance your course cannot continue. You must demonstrate that your eyesight meets the legal minimum requirements using glasses or contact lenses if necessary, before further elements can be taken.

If you use glasses or contact lenses to enable you to read the number plate, you must wear them for the rest of the course and whenever you ride on the road.

What safety issues will I need to know about?

You will need to understand the legal requirements for helmets and how to fasten your helmet securely.

You also need to know about the BSI Kitemark on visors and goggles.

How do I stop my visor from steaming up?

There are anti-fog visors available which can help reduce fogging but if you already have a standard visor you could use an anti-fog spray.

Element B
Practical on-site training

This element provides you with an introduction to the motorcycle. You'll not start riding the motorcycle in this element although you'll get hands-on training.

At the end of this element you'll be able to show a working knowledge of the machine and should have a feel for the weight and balance of a motorcycle.

Motorcycle controls

Your instructor will explain the controls in a logical order. The controls covered include

- **hand controls** - throttle, front brake, clutch, indicators, choke, electric starter, engine cut off or kill switch, lighting switches, horn, fuel tap
- **foot controls** - rear brake, kick starter, gear change lever
- **instruments** - speedometer, rev counter, warning lamps, water temperature and fuel gauges.

Basic skills - Practise finding and using the controls. Some controls are adjustable. Your instructor will explain how they can be set up to suit you.

You'll also need to develop a feel for the controls.

It should not require great strength or force to operate the motorcycle's controls. Be especially careful with the throttle, clutch and brakes.

> **Remember,** that when riding you'll be wearing gloves and boots. This may affect the feel and ease with which you can reach certain controls.

You must be able to operate the controls smoothly and without having to look down to find them.

Basic safety checks and use of the stands

Your instructor will show you how to make basic checks to ensure your motorcycle is safe. These checks will include the

- brakes - correct operation and adjustment
- steering head - wear and adjustment
- control cables - wear, adjustment and lubrication
- fluid levels - hydraulic brake fluid, engine oil, coolant, battery electrolyte
- lights
- suspension
- wheels and spokes
- tyres - wear, damage and pressure
- drive chain - wear, lubrication and tension
- nuts and bolts for tightness
- number plate and reflectors for visibility
- mirrors for clarity.

You will also be shown the types of motorcycle stands and how and when to use them.

Basic skills - While you're not expected to become a motorcycle mechanic, you'll need to be able to recognise basic faults which could affect your motorcycle's roadworthiness.

When using the stands you need to

- demonstrate the correct techniques for putting a motorcycle onto and off its stands
- show an understanding of the effects of camber and gradient.

It's important that you know which machine checks you need to make on a daily basis and which can be left longer.

Make sure you can manage to use the stands correctly. Incorrect methods of using the stands can lead to personal injury or damage to the machine.

Wheeling the motorcycle and braking to stop

You'll learn how to balance a motorcycle while wheeling it both to the left and right (in either order).

Your instructor will show you

- where to stand
- how to hold the motorcycle
- how to lean the motorcycle.

In addition you'll be taught how to use the front brake to stop in a controlled manner. This will involve

- making sure the motorcycle is upright
- practice to get the feel of the front brake.

Basic skills - You'll have to demonstrate

- full control of the motorcycle while wheeling it
- that you have the necessary balance skills.

Your instructor will want to see that you can squeeze the front brake gently and effectively to stop.

When wheeling the motorcycle, avoid

- holding somewhere other than the handlebar grips
- wobbling
- insecure control
- looking down
- harsh use of the front brake.

Starting and stopping the engine

Your instructor will show you what checks you need to make before starting the engine. A mnemonic such as FIGS may be used (see box opposite).

Basic skills - Before starting the engine you'll need to

- be able to find neutral and recognise a 'false neutral'
- demonstrate that you know how to operate the ignition switch and any immobiliser fitted
- know how to operate the starter mechanism fitted to your machine.

Before you start the engine don't forget to turn on the fuel. The engine may well start but will splutter and cut out before you've travelled far if you don't.

Only use the choke for the shortest period necessary. Running with the choke on for longer than you need to can cause

- the engine to run too fast when you're trying to slow down
- increased wear on the engine
- more fuel to be used and more pollution produced.

When starting the engine

- make sure you have selected neutral
- don't hold the kick start lever down after the kick-over
- don't hold the starter button on after the engine has started.

When stopping the engine don't

- use the kill switch unless in an emergency
- forget to switch off the fuel tap (if fitted).

Many motorcycles have a rev counter that shows how fast the engine is running

Fuel

Ignition

Gears

Start

What does FIGS stand for?

Fuel - The use of the choke will be explained and you'll be shown how to

- check for fuel in the tank
- turn on the fuel tap
- use the reserve position.

Ignition - The engine kill switch will be explained and you'll be shown

- the positions on the ignition switch
- how to switch on the ignition.

Gears - Checking for neutral by

- checking the neutral lamp
- rocking the machine back and forward
- spinning the rear wheel on the stand.

Start - You should be shown how to use

- electric starters
- kick starters.

It's important that you know how to operate a kick start but most modern bikes will have electronic starters.

Element C
Practical on-site riding

In this element you'll begin riding a motorcycle. By the time you've finished this element you'll have developed enough basic skills to allow you to ride a motorcycle under control.

You'll learn the essential techniques including rear observation and the Observation - Signal - Manoeuvre (OSM) and Position - Speed - Look (PSL) routines.

You will practise these practical skills until your instructor is satisfied that you'll be safe when you're taken out onto the road.

Riding in a straight line and stopping

This is the point in CBT where you begin riding a motorcycle. Your instructor will explain and may also demonstrate what's required.

You'll be shown how to move off and how to stop. This will include

- using the clutch
- selecting first gear
- finding the 'biting point'
- keeping balance
- using the brakes to stop.

Covering the rear brake will be explained to you and you'll be expected to put this into practice.

Your instructor will also show you how to ride in a straight line, including advice on how to keep your balance.

Basic skills - You'll need to practise until you can

- coordinate the controls when moving off and stopping
- keep your balance
- use both brakes in a smooth and controlled manner.

Try to avoid - When you move off for the first time you may feel insecure. Avoid riding with your feet hanging down. From the beginning learn to ride with your feet up on the footrests.

When you stop you'll have to put a foot down to support the motorcycle. Your instructor will explain which foot to put down. Follow the guidance and make sure you understand why.

Avoid fierce use of the controls at all times as this can lead to stalling the engine, skidding or loss of steering control.

Riding slowly

You'll have to show you can ride a motorcycle slowly and under full control.

This is to prepare you for riding on the road where this skill will be needed to deal with

- junctions
- slow-moving traffic in queues
- hazards.

A demonstration of what is required will probably be given to help show the level of control achievable and how slowly you'll be expected to ride.

Basic skills - You'll need to keep your balance and steering under control while riding slowly.

Try to avoid

- loss of balance
- loss of steering control
- harsh use of throttle and brakes
- riding too fast
- not using the footrests.

Use all of your fingers on the front brake lever for maximum control and stopping power

To begin with you may find it difficult to feel how hard you are pressing the rear brake

Using the brakes

You need to be able to operate the brakes in a controlled manner so that you can

- control your speed
- stop accurately.

You'll be shown how to use both brakes together for maximum control and stopping ability.

The importance of this skill can be related to the need to stop accurately at junctions.

Basic skills - Your instructor will expect you to stop the motorcycle at a marked position. Cones, a line or some other marker may be used to identify where you are expected to stop.

Try to avoid

- stalling as you stop
- use of the rear brake before the front
- use of one brake only
- harsh and late use of the brakes
- locking the wheels
- inaccurate stopping.

What if I brake too hard?

If you brake too hard the affected wheel will lock-up and skid. If this happens you need to release the brake momentarily and then reapply it as firmly as the conditions permit.

What are linked brakes?

Linked braking systems are where the use of one brake control activates both brakes. For maximum braking you will still need to make proper use of both brakes together.

31

Changing gear

You need to be able to change up and down smoothly through the gears.

Your instructor will explain how to operate the controls to achieve smooth gear changes. The space on the training area may limit practice to second or third gear.

Basic skills - You'll need to demonstrate that you can

- coordinate the controls
- make upward and downward gear changes satisfactorily.

Try to avoid

- harsh use of the controls
- failing to coordinate clutch, throttle and gear change lever
- selecting the wrong gear.

Riding a figure of eight

This exercise is to develop steering and balance control when changing from one lock to another.

There are no set size measurements for this exercise. Your instructor may start off with a large layout and reduce it as your skill develops.

Basic skills - You will learn slow speed steering and balance control.

Try to avoid

- riding with your feet off the footrests
- harsh throttle and clutch control
- excessive speed
- wobbling.

Riding a figure of eight around cones will help develop your control, steering and balance while travelling at low speeds

Riding in a figure of eight gives you the chance to practise turning to both left and right at slow speeds in one manoeuvre

Emergency stop

You must be able to stop safely should an emergency arise. Your instructor will explain the effects of applying the brakes individually and using them together.

This may then be followed by a demonstration to highlight the points.

You need to understand

- how weight is transferred during heavy braking
- how weight transfer can affect the rear wheel.

Reference may be made to using the brakes in the ratio 75% front and 25% rear. It's important to understand that this refers to braking force, not lever movement.

You will also need to know about the effects that various weather conditions can have on this braking ratio.

Basic skills - You must be able to coordinate front and rear brakes correctly and in the correct ratio for the conditions.

Try to avoid

- late reactions when signalled to stop
- excessive brake pressure causing either or both wheels to lock
- not responding to the weather and road conditions
- not using the clutch as you stop.

Rear observation

To be safe on the road you should know as much about the traffic behind as you can.

On a motorcycle you can find out about traffic behind by

- using the mirrors
- turning and looking over your shoulder.

Your instructor will explain the special requirements for a motorcyclist including

- how and when to use mirrors
- how to overcome the blind spots.

You should practise looking round before moving off and whilst on the move.

Basic skills - You'll need to practise using your mirrors and looking around while moving so that you can

- see what's behind you
- check blind spots
- keep control whilst looking around.

Try to avoid

- looking round for an excessive time
- veering off course while looking round
- poorly timed rearward glances.

Turning left and right

You need to be able to deal safely with road junctions. Your instructor will explain the OSM (Observation, Signal, Manoeuvre) and PSL (Position, Speed, Look) routines and may give a demonstration.

Use of the mirrors and the 'lifesaver' look will be explained.

An explanation of different junction types, road markings and traffic signals and signs will also be given.

You will need to know how to deal with left and right turns, minor to major and major to minor. A mock junction layout may be set out on the training area for practice.

Basic skills - Right and left turns require different procedures. You need to

- recognise the different types of turn
- demonstrate correct road positioning
- make effective observation
- give correct signals in good time.

Try to avoid

- making badly timed rearward or sideways glances
- giving badly timed or incorrect signals
- looking around when the situation calls for concentration ahead
- not cancelling signals after turning.

Observe

Signal

Position

Look

The skills you gain in this exercise will be needed in both Element E and during the practical motorcycle test

U-turn

Riding a U-turn is a set exercise which also has practical use when riding on the road.

You need to be able to ride your motorcycle around in a U-turn

- under control
- with your feet on the footrests
- keeping aware of the traffic conditions.

Your instructor may demonstrate the level of balance, steering and control needed for this exercise.

You'll be given the chance to practise until you're confident of your ability.

Basic skills - To ride around in a U-turn you need to be able to coordinate and control your

- balance
- steering
- use of the clutch, throttle and rear brake.

In addition you need to understand when, how and where to look for traffic or other hazards.

Try to avoid

- harsh use of the controls
- not taking effective observation
- using your feet to help overcome poor balance.

37

Element D
Practical on-road training

Having carried out theory and practical training off-road, your instructor will now prepare you for the on-road element of CBT. The knowledge you gain now will be the foundations on which to build your motorcycling career.

This element will cover the information you need, to ride legally and safely on the road

During Element E aspects of this theory may be reinforced in practical situations.

Being small, a motorcycle can be difficult to see, especially at some road junctions

At night reflective materials help you to be seen because they shine brightly in the beam of other vehicles' headlights

Conspicuity

It is vitally important to understand why you need to be conspicuous when riding a motorcycle.

Your instructor will discuss why you may not be seen and how you can make it easier for others to see you.

The talk will include

- visibility aids
- differences between fluorescent materials and reflective materials
- use of headlights
- road positioning
- clothing
- keeping your motorcycle clean.

This may be illustrated by a short video presentation.

In addition there will be some discussion on the legal requirements to use dipped headlights in poor visibility.

Making yourself conspicuous is not a legal requirement. However, it's in your own interest to make yourself easier to see. To do so, avoid

- wearing dull clothing
- riding a dirty motorcycle
- riding in another road user's blind area.

Legal requirements

Before you ride on the road there are minimum legal requirements you must be aware of.

Your instructor will explain about

- road tax, insurance and MOT certificates
- provisional motorcycle licence entitlement
- DL196 (CBT completion certificate)
- L plates.

In addition you need to know about general roadworthiness and the legal requirement to fasten your helmet correctly.

Make sure you have all the legal aspects in order before riding on the road. You'll not always be sent a reminder when certain mandatory items need renewal or expire such as

- MOT certificates
- DL196 certificates.

Don't get caught out through neglecting to keep everything up to date.

Routine checks on your motorcycle are necessary to keep it roadworthy

Vulnerability

As a motorcyclist you're generally more vulnerable than other motorists. Your instructor will explain about the dangers of

- falling off
- collision, even at low speed
- weather conditions
- road surface conditions.

The head and limbs are the most exposed parts of your body when riding. Your instructor will tell you what steps you can take to protect yourself from injury and the effects of the weather.

Always buy the best protective equipment you can afford, but don't

- use a helmet that is damaged, second-hand, fits poorly or unfastened
- ride without protective clothing
- ride too fast for the conditions.

Speed

You need to understand why riding at the correct speed is so important. Riding too slowly can be just as much a problem as riding too fast.

> **Remember,** you need to develop a defensive riding style so that you can always stop
>
> - within your range of vision
> - in case a potential hazard turns into a real danger.

Your instructor will explain about the

- legal speed limits
- suitable use of speed
- consequences of speeding and riding too slowly.

Always ride within speed limits and your ability.

41

It is essential that you keep up-to-date, make sure you have a copy of The Highway Code

Anticipating the actions of other road users is a vital part of defensive riding

Highway Code

As a road user you should own a current copy of *The Highway Code* and refer to it often.

Without knowledge of *The Highway Code* you will find it difficult to deal with all aspects of training.

While *The Highway Code* contains all the essential elements of road safety, specific elements relating to CBT will be covered in more detail by your instructor.

Don't treat *The Highway Code* as a book to learn just for your tests. It contains a wealth of information and advice which is designed to keep you safe whenever you use the road.

Refer to it often and follow the advice it gives.

Anticipation

At all times you should ride defensively and anticipate the actions of other road users.

Your instructor will explain that to anticipate you need to

- look well ahead
- plan ahead
- develop hazard awareness
- concentrate at all times.

Remember, anticipation is a skill which develops over time. Signs which show a lack of anticipation include late and harsh braking, being distracted and not taking road and weather conditions into account.

During discussion your instructor will cover a variety of scenarios which illustrate the point being made.

Rear observation

You must understand that rear observation is a combination of using the mirrors and looking around.

Your instructor will explain about

- effective rear observation
- timing of rearward glances
- 'lifesaver' checks.

Some time may be spent discussing the effects of looking around at the wrong moment.

Take care not to

- veer off course while looking round
- look around too late
- look around when you should be concentrating ahead.

Correctly timed rearward glances are an important part of safe riding. Remember, don't lose track of what is developing in front

When passing parked vehicles you need to think about hazards such as doors suddenly opening or oncoming traffic. Take up the correct position so that you can deal with these hazards safely

Road positioning

It's important that you understand where you should position yourself when riding on the road.

Points which will be covered include how you should position yourself to deal with

- bends
- junctions
- road conditions
- single and dual carriageways
- hazards
- overtaking.

When you ride on the road always concentrate and avoid

- riding in the gutter
- erratic steering and veering across your lane
- failing to return to your normal position after dealing with a hazard
- riding on the crown of the road as a normal position.

> **Remember,** when riding around a right hand bend don't let yourself cross onto the opposite side of the road as your motorcycle leans.

Separation distance

You must understand the importance of leaving sufficient space when following another vehicle.

This will involve discussing the advantages of allowing plenty of space such as

- increased ability to see past vehicles ahead and so allow for better forward planning
- increased likelihood of being seen by other road users.

The 'two-second rule' will be explained, and how this is affected by road and weather conditions should be covered.

The special advice for following large vehicles will also be discussed.

Always keep the correct separation distance from the vehicle ahead and allow for the effect road and weather conditions have on your stopping distance. If you are too close behind a large vehicle, the driver might not be able to see you in their mirrors.

Road signs make good markers for using the two-second rule

What are the usual stopping distances?

You should leave enough space between you and the vehicle in front so that you can pull up safely if it suddenly slows or stops.

The safe rule is never to get closer than the overall stopping distances shown below. Don't forget that in wet weather these distances will need to be doubled and can increase up to ten times in icy conditions.

Speed	Thinking	Braking	Distance	
20 mph	6	6	12 metres or 3 car lengths	
30 mph	9	14	23 metres or 6 car lengths	
40 mph	12	24	36 metres or 9 car lengths	
50 mph	15	38	53 metres or 13 car lengths	
60 mph	18	55	73 metres or 18 car lengths	
70 mph	21	75	96 metres or 24 car lengths	

thinking distance

braking distance

Average car length = 4 metres

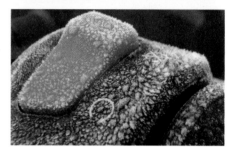

Weather conditions

Motorcyclists are affected more by weather conditions than most other road users.

You can expect some discussion on how these types of weather conditions affect motorcyclists

- low sun
- wind and rain
- fog
- ice, snow and sleet.

In addition your instructor will explain how these weather conditions affect oil spillage, painted road markings and drain covers.

There should be discussion on turbulence caused by large vehicles and the effect that buffeting can have on motorcyclists.

Remember, always respect the effects weather can have when you're riding a motorcycle.

If in doubt, don't set out!

During your training you are unlikely to encounter severe bad weather conditions. When you do find yourself having to ride in bad weather conditions remember the advice your instructor has given.

Road surfaces

You need to be aware of how road conditions can affect a motorcyclist.

There are a variety of road surface hazards which will be explained including

- mud and leaves
- gravel and chippings
- tram and railway lines
- studs
- road markings
- drain covers
- shiny surfaces at junctions and roundabouts.

Clues which can help new riders will be discussed, such as

- rainbow colourings on a wet road indicating oil or fuel spillage
- 'loose chippings' road signs
- mud near farm and field entrances.

Remember, when you're riding always take the road conditions into account, especially when

- cornering
- accelerating
- braking.

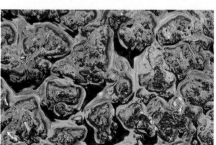

Alcohol and drugs

Alcohol - You're required to know that it's a criminal offence to ride with more than the legal level of alcohol in your blood.

Your instructor will make it clear that despite legally accepted limits, if you want to be safe and you're going to ride, don't drink at all.

The legal limits for riding - Legal riding limits vary across the world, in the UK and Ireland the legal limit is 80 mg/100 ml alcohol content in blood. However, it is always advisable never to drink and ride. Even at the legal limit you have reduced inhibitions.

Drugs - Taking certain drugs when you are going to ride is a criminal offence.

Your instructor will cover

- the effect drugs can have on concentration
- over the counter medicines
- how to check whether any medication will affect your riding ability
- how insurance policies could be invalidated.

Medicine manufacturers label their products to help you identify those that could affect your ability to ride safety. If in doubt ask the chemist or your doctor

Some road users will require particular care and early recognition of the hazard is vital if you are going to respond in good time

Attitude

Your instructor will explain how your attitude can affect your safety. The points raised should include the

- effects of riding while angry
- importance of showing patience
- benefits of riding defensively.

Your attitude is under your control. You could put yourself at additional risk by

- riding while upset or angry
- riding in a spirit of competition on the road
- giving offence or provoking reaction by creating dangerous situations.

Hazard perception

You will be given some idea of what is meant by a hazard.

Remember, always keep up to date with the constantly changing road and traffic situations by concentrating at all times and looking well ahead.

Your instructor will explain

- the importance of planning ahead
- how early recognition makes hazards easier to deal with
- the need for concentration
- the need to use all your senses
- the importance that controlling speed has in dealing with hazards.

Element E

Practical on-road riding

This is the final element of the CBT course. You'll ride out on the road accompanied by, and in radio contact with, a certified instructor, possibly with one other trainee, for at least two hours.

You'll have to demonstrate that you can cope safely with a variety of road and traffic conditions.

Expect your instructor to stop occasionally to discuss some aspect of your riding and explain how to put the theory into practice.

Your ride should cover the topics discussed in this part of the book (some may not be covered because of the limits of the location).

Your riding will be constantly assessed by your instructor, who will sign a certificate of completion (DL196) when satisfied you're safe to continue learning alone.

Those who are profoundly deaf are exempt from the requirement to be in radio contact.

Traffic lights

You must know how to act at traffic lights. Apart from knowing the sequence of lights, you need to know

- what the colours mean
- how to approach green lights safely
- how to cope with filter lanes
- what to do if traffic lights fail.

You'll also need to know about school crossing warning lights.

Basic skills - You must be able to approach traffic lights at the correct speed and react to the road and weather conditions and also react correctly to changing lights.

> ### What is the sequence of the traffic lights
>
> **Red** - Stop and wait at the stop line.
>
> **Red and amber** - Stop and wait. Don't go until green shows.
>
> **Green** - Go, if the way is clear.
>
> **Amber** - Stop, unless you've already crossed the line or you're so close to it that pulling up might cause an accident.

Faults to avoid

- failing to stop at a red light
- approaching green traffic lights too fast
- proceeding into the junction when the green light shows but the way isn't clear
- hesitating as the green light changes and stopping unsafely.

Knowing the sequence of traffic lights can help you plan ahead

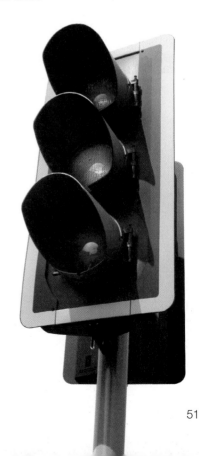

Roundabouts

There are set procedures for dealing with roundabouts. Your instructor should discuss and demonstrate how to go left, ahead and right.

This will involve learning how to apply the OSM/PSL routine for the direction you intend to travel. This will include

- signalling procedures
- lane discipline
- observation.

Your instructor will want to see you use the correct procedures for each roundabout you deal with.

Basic skills - You must be able to

- take effective rear observation
- approach at the correct speed and judge the speed of other traffic
- give the correct signals at the right time and cancel them correctly
- follow the correct road position throughout.

Faults to avoid

- giving wrong or misleading signals
- approaching at the wrong speed
- stopping when the way is clear or riding out into the path of approaching traffic
- positioning incorrectly
- failing to take effective observation.

Junctions

You'll have practised turning left and right in Element C. You'll now have to combine those riding skills with real traffic situations.

Your instructor will want to see you deal with a variety of junctions. These may include

- crossroads
- T-junctions
- staggered junctions
- Y-junctions.

You'll be expected to respond to signs such as

- warning signs
- 'stop' signs
- direction signs
- 'no entry' signs
- priority signs.

Don't forget to also take account of the road markings.

> **Remember,** the road surface at junctions is often an additional hazard for motorcyclists. If you're riding on a shiny or loose surface don't
>
> - brake fiercely
> - accelerate harshly.

You must show you're aware of other road users and watch for vehicles approaching, emerging or turning.

Basic skills - To deal safely with junctions you must

- use the OSM/PSL routine correctly as you approach a junction
- position yourself correctly on the road
- control your speed to suit the road, weather and traffic conditions
- obey road signs and markings
- react correctly to other road users
- demonstrate effective observation.

Your instructor will make sure you can deal safely with all types of junctions

Faults to avoid - All junctions must be treated with great care. Avoid

- stopping or waiting unnecessarily
- approaching a junction too fast
- overtaking as you approach a junction
- riding into a junction unsafely
- incorrect use of signals
- incorrect road position.

Zebra crossings have beacons to help you see the crossing from a distance

Pelican, Puffin and Toucan crossings are activated when someone pushes the button

Pedestrian crossings

There's a variety of pedestrian crossings you may encounter

- zebra
- pelican
- toucan
- puffin.

Your instructor will want to see you deal with crossings in the appropriate way

- zebra crossings - slow down and be prepared to stop for waiting pedestrians
- pelican and puffin - always stop if the red light shows. You should also give way to pedestrians on a pelican crossing when the amber lights are flashing
- toucan crossings - don't forget to give way to cyclists on a toucan crossing, as you would to pedestrians.

Basic skills - As you approach a crossing you need to

- control your speed
- react correctly to pedestrians waiting to cross
- know how and why you would give an arm signal as you stop at a zebra crossing.

Faults to avoid

- approaching a crossing too fast
- failing to stop or show awareness of waiting pedestrians
- stopping across a crossing so blocking the way for pedestrians
- overtaking within the zigzag lines leading up to a crossing
- waving pedestrians across the road
- failing to respond correctly to traffic light signals at controlled crossings.

Gradients

During this element your instructor will want to see that you can cope with gradients.

This will entail

- hill start procedures
- riding uphill
- riding downhill.

You should have some understanding of how riding uphill or downhill can affect control of your motorcycle.

> **Remember**, when riding up a steep hill you need to be able to match the gear to the speed and load on the engine.

Basic skills - To move off on an uphill gradient you need to have good control of the clutch and throttle

Steeper gradients have warning signs that show how steep the hill is and which way it slopes

When riding down a steep hill you need to know how to control your speed using the brakes and gears

Faults to avoid

- moving off into the path of passing traffic
- stalling the engine
- rolling backwards.

55

Bends

Any bend can be a hazard. You must be able to recognise the hazard and deal with it safely.

Your instructor will want to see that you ride at a speed such that you can stop within the distance you can see and keep to the correct road position. Also that you are aware of road surface hazards such as drain covers, loose surfaces and adverse camber.

On left-hand bends you will have less view ahead. Be prepared for pedestrians, stopped or broken down vehicles, cyclists and stopped vehicles waiting to turn right.

You should know how the weather affects your safety when cornering.

Basic skills - To help you assess any bend you should be looking out for road signs, road markings and chevrons.

When approaching a bend, you need to control your speed and select the correct gear, also you must leave a safe gap between you and other vehicles. You must also be able to lean into a bend while steering a steady course.

Faults to avoid

- braking while leaning over
- coasting
- cornering too fast
- leaning over too far
- riding too close to oncoming traffic or too close to the gutter.

Your instructor will give you guidance to help you position correctly for right and left bends

Advance warning triangles help you to plan ahead even though you may not be able to see the obstruction

A bus is a large and obvious obstruction and its size could also make it easy to conceal people wanting to cross the road

Obstructions

Obstructions are another hazard you will need to deal with.

To deal safely with these your instructor will want to see that you're riding defensively.

That's always riding

- at the correct speed for the road, weather and traffic conditions
- in the correct position
- in the correct gear
- looking ahead, anticipating and preparing for changing situations.

Basic skills - How well you cope with an obstruction depends largely on how well you plan ahead.

To cope with hazards you need to be

- looking well ahead
- giving yourself time and space to react
- using the OSM/PSL routine
- in the correct position
- in full control of your speed.

Your attitude can affect how easily you learn these skills.

Faults to avoid

- failing to look far enough ahead
- reacting too late
- riding too fast
- approaching an obstruction in the wrong gear.

U-turn

As part of Element C you practised riding a U-turn on the training area. During this element you'll be expected to ride a U-turn on the road. This builds on the skills you learned earlier and helps prepare you for your practical motorcycle test.

Your instructor will find a quiet side road and explain what's required.

You cannot complete Element E until your instructor is satisfied you can safely ride a U-turn on the road.

Basic skills - You'll need to show you have developed good balance and are skilled in the use of the clutch, throttle, rear brake and steering.

You'll have to develop these skills to include coping with

- the camber of the road
- the possibility of passing traffic
- kerbs on either side.

Faults to avoid

- failure to take effective observation before or during the exercise
- riding into the kerb or onto the pavement
- using your feet to help balance
- harsh, clumsy use of the clutch and throttle.

Stopping as in an emergency

You've learnt and practised this exercise in Element C.

In this element you repeat the exercise but in an on-road situation. This will

- develop your earlier skills
- help ensure your safety if an emergency does arise
- prepare you for performing this exercise on your practical motorcycle test.

Your instructor will find a quiet side road and explain the signal to be used.

You'll then be expected to ride at normal speed before being given the signal to stop.

At no time will your instructor let you ride off out of sight.

Basic skills

- quick reaction to the 'stop' signal
- use of both brakes in the appropriate ratio
- the ability to quickly correct a locked wheel.

Faults to avoid

- riding too slowly before the signal
- taking rear observation before reacting to the stop signal
- locking one or both wheels and failing to correct the fault
- stopping too slowly
- moving off unsafely after stopping.

CBT record

Name		has satisfactorily completed:

	Signature of instructor	Date of completion
Element A Introduction to CBT		
Element B Practical on-site training		
Element C Practical on-site riding		
Element D Practical on-road training		
Element E Practical on-road riding		

Name of ATB	

Using the record

You can use this log to record your progress through CBT. As you successfully complete each element get your instructor to sign this progress record.

This will give you

- a record of when you successfully complete each element
- a record of your instructor
- evidence of your progress to date.

After CBT

CBT will give you the foundations on which to build a safe motorcycling career. However, like all new skills you need training and practice to become good at them.

Training

Many ATBs provide additional training up to practical test standard. When you attend this training you may find you are in a group with other learners.

There is a maximum ratio of four learners to each instructor for post CBT training using learner machines.

Sometimes ATBs can book your theory and practical tests for you. Ask your instructor about further training and make sure the full syllabus is covered (see section six).

Practice

This is essential so that you practise

- on as many types of road as you can
- on dual carriageways where the national speed limit applies
- in all sorts of conditions (even in darkness).

You'll be asked to ride on a variety of road types during the test. Don't just concentrate on roads near the test centre or the exercises included in the test. When you practise try not to

- obstruct other traffic. Most drivers are tolerant of learners, but don't try their patience too much
- annoy local residents. For example, by practising emergency stops in quiet residential streets.

In busy urban conditions you may have to consider many hazards close together. Prioritising hazards is a skill that develops with practice

Rural roads present some unique hazards but concentration and good forward planning should enable you to deal with them safely

61

section **three**

BEFORE YOUR TEST

This section covers
- Booking your tests
- Your theory test
- Theory into practice
- The practical test
- Your test motorcycle

Booking your tests

Some ATBs will be able to book your theory and practical test for you. Alternatively, you can book your tests online, by telephone, or by post as explained below.

Booking online or by telephone

You can book theory and practical tests by either of these methods and you'll be given the date and time of your test immediately.

You can book online at www.direct.gov.uk/drivingtest.

To book by telephone, call 0870 0101 372. If you are deaf and need a minicom machine telephone 0870 0107 372 and if you are a Welsh speaker you can telephone 0870 0100 372. To book in Northern Ireland call 0845 600 6700 for theory tests or 0870 247 2471 for practical tests.

When booking you'll need to identify what sort of test you want to book and provide

- your driver number (from your licence)
- credit or debit card details. Please note that the person who books the test must be the card holder
- if booking a practical test you will need your theory test pass certificate number.

You'll be given a booking number and sent an appointment letter within a few days.

Booking by post

Fill in the application form for the type of test you wish to take and send it, together with the correct fee, to the address shown on the back of the form. You can get application forms from driving test centres or ask your ATB.

You may pay by cheque, postal order or with credit/debit card. Please do not send cash. You'll receive an appointment letter within 10 days.

The easiest way to book your test is online. Simply visit www.direct.gov.uk/drivingtest

Appointment letter

Whether you book your test online, by telephone or by post you will receive an appointment letter to take with you when you go for your test. It will include

- the time and place of your test
- the address of the test centre

Disabilities or special needs

Whichever test you book, you need to let them know if you have a disability or if there are any other special circumstances. You will still take the same type of test as every other test candidate, but more time may be allowed for the test.

To make sure enough time is allowed, it would help DSA to know if you

- are deaf or have severe hearing difficulties
- are in any way restricted in your movements
- have any disability which may affect your riding.

If you can't speak English or are deaf, you are allowed to bring an interpreter (who must not be an instructor). The interpreter must be 16 years or over.

How much do the tests cost?

Your ATB should be able to tell you or you can find out from www.direct.gov.uk/drivingtest or by calling 0870 0101 372.

Can I take my tests on a weekend or in the evening?

Theory tests are available on some weekday evenings and Saturdays while practical tests are available at some test centres on Saturdays, Sundays and in the summer, on weekday evenings. The fee for practical tests taken outside normal working hours is higher than during normal working hours on weekdays.

How do I change or cancel my test appointment?

You can change or cancel your test appointment online at www.direct.gov.uk/drivingtest. Alternatively, you can change or cancel a test appointment by calling 0870 0101 372.

You need to give at least three clear working days notice for change or cancellation of a theory or practical test, not counting the day DSA receive your request and the day of the test (Saturday is counted as a working day). If you don't give enough notice you'll lose your fee.

Your theory test

At theory test centres lockers are provided for your personal possessions

Your result should be available within ten minutes of completing the test

The theory test will gauge your knowledge and understanding of riding theory and hazard perception.

A sound knowledge of the theory is essential to a better understanding of practical riding skills.

Who's affected?

All motorcycle test candidates will have to pass the theory test before a booking for a practical test will be accepted. However, you will not have to take a theory test if you hold a full moped licence obtained by passing both a theory and practical moped test or are upgrading your motorcycle licence from an A1 to category A.

Ready for your test?

If you are well prepared you won't find the questions difficult. *The Official DSA Theory Test for Motorcyclists* is available as a book or on CD-Rom, it contains comprehensive information about the test and all the multiple choice questions, answers and explanations.

Study your copy of *The Highway Code* and the publications *The Official DSA Guide to Riding - the essential skills* and *Know Your Traffic Signs*. Always make sure that you have the most up-to-date versions of these books.

It's very important that you know why the answers to the multiple choice questions are correct. Take this knowledge and put it into practice on the road. Your examiner will expect you to demonstrate what you have learned through your riding.

Hazard perception

We strongly recommend that you use *The Official Guide to Hazard Perception* (DVD) preferably with your instructor, to prepare for the hazard perception part of the theory test. Alternatively, this is available as a VHS and booklet pack.

The DVD is packed with useful tips, quizzes and expert advice. It also includes interactive hazard perception clips, with feedback on your performance.

It's important that you study, not just to pass the test, but to become a safer rider

On the day

The test centre staff will check your documents. You'll have to show your driving licence, and if your licence doesn't show your photograph you will also have to show your passport (your passport doesn't have to be British). No other form of identification is acceptable.

Other forms of identification may be acceptable in Northern Ireland, please check www.dvani.gov.uk or refer to your test appointment letter.

All documents must be original. We can't accept photocopies.

Arrive in plenty of time so that you aren't rushed. If you arrive late you may not be allowed to take the test.

If you pass

The result should be available within 10 minutes of completing your test. If you've passed you'll be issued with a pass certificate. Take it with you when you go for your practical test. This certificate will be valid for two years. You must take and pass the practical test within that time or you'll have to take the theory test again.

If you fail

If you haven't passed the theory test then you must retake it. You'll have to wait a minimum of three clear working days before you take the test again.

Theory into practice

When you take your practical test you must satisfy your examiner that you have fully understood everything which you learned for the theory test. The aspects are

- alertness and concentration
- courtesy and consideration
- care in the use of the controls to reduce mechanical wear and tear
- awareness of stopping distances and safety margins in all conditions
- hazard awareness
- correct action concerning pedestrians and other vulnerable road users
- dealing with other types of vehicle in the correct manner
- rules regarding speed limits and stopping restrictions
- road and traffic signs.

You will also be expected to know

- the law regarding you and your vehicle
- what to do in the event of an accident
- the effect extra loads have on your vehicle
- the effect motoring has on the environment
- how to carry out simple safety checks on your vehicle.

The practical test

About the practical test

The practical test is designed to assess whether you can ride safely. The test ensures that all riders reach a minimum standard. You will pass the test if you can show your examiner that you can

- ride safely and competently
- complete the special exercises
- demonstrate through your riding that you have a thorough knowledge of *The Highway Code*.

During the test your examiner will follow you either on a motorcycle or in a car. You will be fitted with earphones under your helmet and a radio receiver on a waist belt. This will enable you to hear the examiner's directions while riding on the road. You'll be given directions clearly and in good time.

Your test will be carried out over a route covering a wide variety of road and traffic conditions and will include

- an eyesight test (see p73)
- two questions about carrying out safety checks on the vehicle (see p74)
- special exercises, such as an emergency stop (see p84).

At the end of the test your examiner will ask you a question about carrying a pillion passenger on your machine. Throughout the test you should demonstrate the knowledge you have gained from studying for your theory test

How long will the test last?

The test lasts about 40 minutes.

Are examiners supervised?

Examiners are frequently supervised by a senior officer. If a senior officer is present at your test, don't worry. They are only there to check that your examiner is testing you properly and won't interfere with the test or the result. They are not there to test you in any way.

How should I ride on the test?

The examiner will be looking for an overall safe ride. If you make a mistake, don't worry, it might not affect the result.

Does the standard of the test vary?

No. All examiners are trained to carry out tests to the same standard. Test routes are as uniform as possible and include a range of typical road and traffic conditions.

How the examiner records faults

Total S D

① ② ③④

Total Faults ⑤

① **Driving fault -** A less serious fault, but an accumulation of these may result in failure

② **Area total -** The number of driving faults made in one area

③ **Serious fault -** Committing one of these will result in failure

④ **Dangerous fault -** Committing one of these will result in failure

⑤ **Overall total -** The total number of driving faults made in all areas during the test

On the day

Your examiner will be understanding and sympathetic and will make every effort to put you at ease.

You'll have to show your driving licence, and if your licence doesn't show your photograph you'll also have to show your passport (your passport doesn't have to be British). No other form of identification is acceptable. Other forms of identification may be acceptable in Northern Ireland, please check www.dvani.gov.uk or refer to your test appointment letter.

Your examiner will also need to see your CBT completion certificate unless you are upgrading your full motorcycle entitlement.

How you will be assessed

Your examiner will assess any errors you make and, depending on their degree of seriousness, record them on the Driving Test Report form (DL25). You will fail your test if you commit a serious or dangerous fault. You will also fail if you commit more than a fixed number of driving faults. The examiner will use following criteria:

Driving fault - Less serious, but has been assessed as such because of circumstances at that particular time. An accumulation of more than a fixed number of driving faults will result in a fail.

Serious fault - Recorded when a potentially dangerous incident has occurred or a habitual driving fault indicates a serious weakness in a your riding.

Dangerous fault - Recorded when a fault is assessed as having caused actual danger.

At the end of the test you will be offered some general guidance to explain your Driving Test Report.

Are you ready?

If you've taken additional training, be guided by your instructor, who has the knowledge and experience to tell you when you're ready.

You must be able to ride consistently well and with confidence, without assistance and guidance from your instructor.

If you can't, you aren't ready for the test. Waiting until you are ready will save you time and money.

Can anyone accompany me on the test?

If you need an interpreter you should notify DSA in advance and arrange for the interpreter to meet you at the test centre. Your interpreter must be 16 years or over and you may not use an approved instructor for that purpose.

The Data Protection Act prevents your instructor from talking to your examiner about your practical test without your permission. If you did not pass your test and want your instructor to help you understand the reason(s) why, your instructor needs to be on hand at the end of the test to listen to the debrief that the examiner will offer you. Tell the examiner that you would like your instructor to be present. This can help your instructor to plan any further training that you might need.

Passing the test

You'll pass if you can satisfy the examiner that you can ride safely, comply with correct road procedure, obey traffic signs and carry out the special exercises correctly.

When you've passed

You'll be allowed to ride without L plates, unsupervised and on motorways.

The size of motorcycle you'll be licensed to ride immediately after passing your test will depend on the machine you've used to take the test. See the next page for test motorcycle requirements.

Your test motorcycle

75-125cc - To obtain a light motorcycle licence

121-125cc (capable of at least 100km/h) - To obtain a standard motorcycle licence

35kW minimum - For direct and accelerated access

Use the following checklist to make sure that the motorcycle you intend to use for you test will be acceptable.

Legally roadworthy - Your machine must have a current test certificate, if it's over the prescribed age.

Insurance - You must be fully covered by insurance for you to ride on the date of your test and for its present use.

Size and power - Ensure that your machine has the correct engine size/power output for the category of test that you're taking.

Licence - Make sure that your motorcycle is properly licensed with the correct tax disc on display.

L plates - The L plates (or D plates in Wales) fitted to your bike must be visible from the front and rear.

If you overlook any of these your test may be cancelled and you could lose your fee.

What else should I know about test motorcycles?

Motorcycles less than 75 cc aren't acceptable.

Only the disabled can use a motorcycle and sidecar combination for the test. The licence obtained will be restricted to such combinations.

What if I use a machine with automatic transmission?

If you pass your test on a motorcycle with automatic or semi-automatic transmission this will be recorded on your licence.

This will mean that your full licence entitlement will be restricted to motorcycles in this category.

section **four**
THE PRACTICAL RIDING TEST

This section covers

- The eyesight test
- Safety checks
- Before you start the engine
- The motorcycle controls
- Moving off
- Rear observation
- Giving signals
- Acting on signs and signal
- Use of speed
- Making progress
- The emergency stop
- Special exercises
- Hazards
- Selecting a safe place to stop
- Awareness and anticipation

The eyesight test

What the test requires

You must satisfy your examiner that, in good daylight, you can read a vehicle number plate with letters 79.4 mm (3.1 inches) high at a minimum distance of 20.5 metres (about 67 feet).

Number plates in the format (XX50XXX) have a narrower font and should be read from a distance of 20 metres (66 feet).

You will be asked to read a clean number plate in good daylight

If you need glasses or contact lenses to read the number plate, that is fine. However, you must wear them during the test and whenever you ride.

If you have had sight correction surgery you should declare this when you apply for your provisional licence.

How your examiner will test you

Before you begin riding, your examiner will point out a vehicle and ask you to read its number plate.

> **Remember,** if you normally wear glasses or contact lenses, always wear them whenever you ride.

If you can't speak English or have difficulty reading, you may copy down what you see.

If your answer is incorrect, your examiner will measure the exact distance and repeat the test.

Failing the eyesight test

If you can't show your examiner that your eyesight is up to the required standard

- you will have failed your motorcycle test
- your test will go no further.

Safety checks

What the test requires

You must satisfy the examiner that you're capable of preparing to ride safely by carrying out simple safety checks on the motorcycle you're using on the test.

You will be expected to know how to carry out checks relating to

- tyres
- brakes
- fluids
- lights
- reflectors
- direction indicators
- horn.

How your examiner will test you

At the start of the test the examiner will ask you to explain and demonstrate how you would carry out certain safety checks.

What your examiner is looking for - The examiner wants to see that you're familiar with the motorcycle you're using for the test.

They will want you to explain, and in some cases demonstrate, how you would carry out simple safety checks on the motorcycle you're using on the test.

What you can be asked about

The examiner could ask you about checking

- tyres for correct pressure and condition
- brakes for working order before any journey
- fluid levels (including engine oil, brake fluid and, on a motorcycle with a liquid cooled engine, coolant) - where they are and how you would check the levels
- reflectors and lights (including brake lights and direction indicators) for good working order and visibility
- the drive chain (if fitted) for wear, lubrication and tension
- the engine kill switch
- other components (including steering, horn and warning devices) for good working order.

There is only a limited number of safety check questions that you can be asked on test. They can all be found on www.direct.gov.uk/motoring

Faults you should avoid - Being unable to explain or demonstrate basic safety checks on the motorcycle you're using for the test.

Before you start the engine

What the test requires

Before you start the engine you must always check that

- the fuel tap is turned on
- the engine kill switch is in the 'on' position
- the gear lever is in neutral.

Many road safety organisations recommend that you use dipped headlights at all times. **Be seen, be safe.**

Faults to avoid - You shouldn't

- use the fuel tap's reserve position instead of the 'on' position. The motorcycle will run normally but you'll have no warning when your fuel is running low.
- use the clutch to allow you to start the engine without first having found neutral.

The motorcycle controls

What the test requires

You should understand the functions of all switches which have a bearing on road safety such as your indicators, horn and lights. You should know where to find these switches on the motorcycle you are riding.

You should also understand the meaning of gauges or other instruments including the speedometer and various warning lights.

You are also required to know the functions of all controls including

- throttle
- clutch
- front and rear brake
- steering
- gears.

You should use these controls

- smoothly
- competently
- safely
- at the right time.

If you are riding an automatic - Make sure that you fully understand the controls before you attempt to ride a motorcycle with automatic transmission.

Throttle and clutch

You should

- balance the throttle and clutch to pull away smoothly
- accelerate gradually to gain speed
- pull the clutch in just before the motorcycle stops.

If you're riding a motorcycle with automatic or semi-automatic transmission, you should ensure that the brakes are used to prevent creeping forward and control the throttle when moving off and changing gear.

Faults to avoid - Don't accelerate fiercely. This can lead to a loss of control and may distract or alarm other road users.

Avoid using the clutch in a jerky and uncontrolled manner when moving off or changing gear.

Brakes

You should use both brakes correctly and in good time. You should brake lightly in most situations.

Faults to avoid - You shouldn't brake harshly, except in an emergency. Use either the front or rear brake alone.

You should understand all the instruments and know what to do if a warning light is showing

Gears

You should choose the right gear for your speed and road conditions. Change gear in good time so that you are ready for a hazard or junction.

Faults to avoid - You shouldn't

- select the wrong gear
- coast with the clutch lever pulled in or the gear lever in neutral.

Steering

You should keep both hands on the handlebars and make sure your steering movements are steady and smooth.

Always begin turning at the correct time when negotiating a corner and show awareness of the road surface.

Faults to avoid - Don't turn too early when steering around a corner. If you do, you risk

- cutting the corner when turning right and putting others at risk
- striking the kerb when turning left.

Don't turn too late. You could put other road users at risk by swinging wide on left turns and overshooting right turns.

You shouldn't brake and steer together, lean the motorcycle over too far and cause one or both tyres to lose their grip or move out before turning left.

Moving off

What the test requires

You should be able to move off

- safely
- under control
- on the flat
- from behind a parked car
- on a hill, where appropriate.

Before moving off you will need to look around and check for hazards that would not be visible in your mirrors

How your examiner will test you

Your examiner will watch your use of the controls and observation of other road users each time you move off.

Use your mirrors and signal if necessary.

Before you move off, look around over your shoulder and check any blind spots that can't be seen in your mirror. Check for

- traffic
- pedestrians.

Move off under control making balanced use of the

- throttle
- clutch
- brakes
- steering.

You should also ensure that you move off in the correct gear.

Faults to avoid - You shouldn't

- immediately signal without first taking effective observation around you
- pull out without looking
- cause other road users to stop or alter their course
- accelerate excessively
- move off in too high a gear
- fail to coordinate the controls correctly and stall the engine.

Rear observation

Looking around while moving needs to be timed carefully and performed without affecting the steering

What the test requires

Make sure that you take effective rear observation

- before any manoeuvre
- to keep aware of what is happening behind you.

Check carefully before

- moving off
- signalling
- changing direction
- turning to the left or right
- overtaking or changing lanes
- increasing speed
- slowing down or stopping.

How your examiner will test you

Your examiner will watch your use of rear observation as you ride. Use the OSM routine. You should

- look before you signal
- look and signal before you act
- act sensibly and safely on what you see when you have taken rear observation.

You should be aware that the mirrors won't show everything behind you (see page 35 for more information about blind spots).

Faults to avoid - You shouldn't manoeuvre without taking rear observation or fail to act on what you see behind.

Giving signals

What the test requires

You should signal

- to let others know what you intend to do
- to help other road users, including pedestrians
- in plenty of time.

You must only use the signals shown in *The Highway Code*.

Your signals should help other road users

- to understand what you intend to do
- to react safely.

Always make sure that your signal is cancelled after use.

How your examiner will test you

Your examiner will watch carefully how you use your signals as you ride.

Give signals clearly and in good time.

You should also know how to give arm signals and when they are necessary.

Faults to avoid - You shouldn't

- give signals carelessly
- mislead other road users
- forget to cancel the signal
- wave at pedestrians to cross the road.

Acting on signs and signals

What the test requires

You should be able to understand all traffic signs and road markings. You must also react to them in good time.

At the beginning of the test your examiner will ask you to follow the road ahead.

You will be **asked** to turn at junctions, but look out for lane markings and direction signs. You will be expected to act on these.

Traffic lights - You must act correctly at traffic lights. When the green light shows, check that the road is clear before proceeding.

Signals by authorised persons - You must obey the signals given by

- police officers
- traffic wardens
- school crossing patrols.
- Highway Agency Traffic officers and Vehicle and Operator Services Agency officers.

Traffic calming measures - Take particular care on roads which have been altered by the addition of

- 20 mph speed limit zones
- speed restriction humps
- width restrictions marked by bollards, posts or paved areas.

Use of speed

What the test requires

You should make good progress along the road bearing in mind

- road conditions
- traffic conditions
- weather conditions
- road signs and speed limits.

How your examiner will test you

Your examiner will watch carefully your control of speed as you ride. You should

- take great care in the use of speed
- make sure that you can stop safely, well within the distance you can see to be clear

- leave a safe distance between yourself and other vehicles
- leave extra distance on wet or slippery roads
- approach junctions and hazards at the correct speed.

Faults to avoid - You shouldn't

- ride too fast for the road and traffic conditions
- change your speed unpredictably.

Making progress

What the test requires

You should

- make reasonable progress along the road
- drive at a speed appropriate to road and traffic conditions
- move off at junctions as soon as it's safe to do so.

How your examiner will test you

Your examiner will watch your riding and will want to see you

- make reasonable progress along the road
- keep up with traffic
- show confidence, together with sound judgement
- comply with the speed limits.

You should be able to choose the correct speed for the

- type of road
- road surface
- type and density of traffic
- weather and visibility.

Faults to avoid - You shouldn't

- drive too slowly, holding up other traffic
- be over-cautious or stop and wait when it's safe to go
- prepare too early for junctions by approaching too slowly and holding up traffic.

Remember, you should approach all hazards at a safe speed.

83

The emergency stop

The signal to stop will be clear and only given when there is no danger to or from other traffic

What the test requires

In an emergency you should be able to stop the motorcycle

- as quickly as possible
- safely and under control
- without locking the wheels.

How your examiner will test you

Your examiner will ask you to stop at the side of the road. They will then explain the procedure and demonstrate the signal to you. When your examiner gives the signal, try to stop the motorcycle as you would in a real emergency.

You should react quickly and try to stop in a straight line. Don't forget to take special care if the road is wet.

Your examiner will check that the road is clear behind you before the signal is given.

You should stop the motorcycle

- in a short distance
- under full control
- without risk to other road users.

Faults to avoid - You shouldn't anticipate the signal by slowing or stopping while your examiner is checking the road behind. You should also avoid skidding out of control or pulling up slowly.

Special exercises

Walking with your machine

Your examiner will ask you to put your machine on its stand. You will then be asked to take the machine off its stand and to walk with it, normally in a U-turn, but without the aid of the engine.

Riding a U-turn

Your examiner will ask you to ride a U-turn. Direct rear observation into the blind area is vital just before you carry out the turn.

Angle start

Your examiner will ask you to pull up just before a parked vehicle. Before you move off, make sure that you check

- to the rear and into the blind area
- ahead to see there is no danger from approaching traffic.

If an angle start occurs normally during the test, you may not be asked to do it again.

Slow ride

You will be asked to ride along at walking speed for a short distance. This tests your control, balance and observation. If you have already ridden slowly, such as in traffic, you may not be asked to carry out this exercise.

Hill start

Your examiner might ask you to pull up on an uphill gradient.

When moving off, your machine could be slower to accelerate. You will need to remember this when judging the moment to ride off.

Balance question

After the practical part of the test your examiner will ask you one question about balance when carrying a pillion passenger.

Keep a look out for approaching traffic whilst you walk the machine in a U-turn

85

Hazards - the correct routine

What is a hazard?

A hazard is any situation which could involve adjusting speed or altering course. Look well ahead where there are

- road junctions or roundabouts
- parked vehicles
- cyclists or horse riders
- pedestrian crossings.

By identifying the hazard early you will have time to take the appropriate action.

You may have to deal with several hazards at once or during a short space of time. This may mean using your initiative and common sense to deal with the particular circumstances.

What the test requires

Always use the OSM/PSL routine when approaching a hazard.

Observation - Check the position of following traffic using your mirrors or by looking behind at an appropriate time.

Signal - If necessary, signal your intention to change course or slow down. Signal clearly and in good time.

Manoeuvre - A manoeuvre is any change of speed or position, from slowing or stopping to turning off a busy road. Manoeuvre has three phases; position, speed, then look. You should consider each phase in turn and use them as appropriate.

Junctions and roundabouts

What the test requires

You should

- use the OSM routine when you approach a junction or a roundabout
- position your motorcycle correctly. Adjust your speed and stop if necessary
- use the correct lane if the road has lane markings. In a one-way street choose that lane as soon as you can do so safely.

If the road has no lane markings, when turning left, keep to the left.

Watch out for

- cyclists
- pedestrians crossing.

When turning right, you should

- keep as close to the centre of the road as is safe
- use effective observation before you enter a junction
- make a 'lifesaver' check over your right shoulder before you turn.

How your examiner will test you

Your examiner will watch carefully and take account of your

- use of the OSM/PSL routine
- position and speed on approach to the hazard
- observation and judgement.

You should be able to

- observe road signs and markings and act correctly on what you see
- judge the correct speed on approach to the hazard
- slow down in good time, without harsh braking
- judge the speed of the other traffic, especially at roundabouts and when you are joining major roads
- position and turn correctly.

Faults to avoid - You shouldn't

- approach the junction at the wrong speed
- position and turn incorrectly
- enter a junction unsafely
- stop or wait unnecessarily.

Overtaking

What the test requires

When overtaking you must

- observe any signs and road markings which prohibit overtaking
- allow enough room
- give cyclists and horses at least as much room as a car. Cyclists might swerve or wobble and a startled horse can shy or jump unpredictably
- allow enough space after overtaking. Don't cut in.

If you need to overtake use the OSM/PSL routine. Don't overtake when approaching a junction as the driver could be turning right and may not be aware of you

How your examiner will test you

Your examiner will watch and take into account how you

- use the OSM/PSL routine
- react to road and traffic conditions
- handle the controls.

You should be able to judge the speed and position of vehicles

- behind, which might be trying to overtake you
- in front, if you are planning to overtake
  - coming towards you.

    Overtake only when you can do so

    - safely
    - without causing other vehicles to slow down or alter course.

    Faults to avoid - You shouldn't overtake when

- your view of the road ahead isn't clear
- you would have to exceed the speed limit
- there is oncoming traffic and you are squeezing between the oncoming traffic and the vehicle you are overtaking
- the road is narrow.

Meeting and passing other vehicles

What the test requires

You should deal with oncoming traffic safely and confidently. This applies on narrow roads and where there are parked cars or other obstructions.

If there is an obstruction on your side of the road, or not enough space for two vehicles to pass safely, you should use the OSM/PSL routine and be prepared to give way to oncoming traffic.

If you need to stop, keep well back from the obstruction to give yourself

- a better view of the road ahead
- room to move off easily when the road is clear.

When you are passing parked cars, allow at least the width of a car door, if possible.

How your examiner will test you

Your examiner will watch carefully and take into account how you

- use the OSM/PSL routine
- react to road and traffic conditions
- handle the controls.

Be patient. Don't be tempted to squeeze through small gaps

You should

- show judgement and control when meeting oncoming traffic
- be decisive when stopping and moving off
- allow enough room when passing parked cars.

Watch out for

- doors opening
- children running out into the road
- pedestrians stepping out from the pavement
- vehicles pulling out without warning.

Crossing the path of other vehicles

What the test requires

You should be able to cross the path of other vehicles safely and with confidence.

You normally need to cross the path of other vehicles when you have to turn right into a side road or driveway. You should

- use the OSM/PSL routine
- position correctly and adjust your speed
- watch out for oncoming traffic and stop if necessary.

Watch out for pedestrians crossing the side road or on the pavement, if you are entering a driveway.

How your examiner will test you

Your examiner will watch carefully and take account of your judgement of the oncoming traffic.

You should show that you can turn right into a junction or driveway safely, using the OSM/PSL routine.

Faults to avoid - You shouldn't cause other vehicles to slow down, swerve or stop.

You shouldn't

- turn too early and cut the corner
- leave it too late before you start to turn.

Following behind at a safe distance

What the test requires

You should always ride so that you can stop within the distance you can see to be clear.

Always keep a safe distance between yourself and the vehicle in front.

In good conditions, leave a gap of at least one metre (just over three feet) for every mile per hour you are travelling. Or leave a two-second time gap.

In bad conditions, leave at least double the distance, or a four-second time gap.

In slow-moving, congested traffic it may not be practical to leave so much space.

How your examiner will test you

Your examiner will watch carefully and take account of how you

- use the OSM/PSL routine
- anticipate situations
- react to changing road and traffic conditions
- handle the controls.

You should

- be able to judge a safe separation distance between you and the vehicle in front
- show correct use of the OSM/PSL routine, especially before reducing speed
- avoid the need to brake harshly if the vehicle in front slows down or stops
- take extra care when your view ahead is limited by large vehicles such as lorries or buses.

Watch out for

- brake lights ahead
- direction indicators
- vehicles ahead braking without warning.

Faults to avoid - You shouldn't

- follow too closely
- brake suddenly
- stop too close to the vehicle in front in a traffic queue.

Positioning and lane discipline

What the test requires

You should

- normally keep well to the left
- keep clear of parked vehicles
- avoid weaving in and out between parked vehicles
- position your vehicle correctly for the direction you intend to take.

You should obey all lane markings, for example, bus and cycle lanes. In one-way streets be particularly aware of left or right turn lane arrows at junctions.

How your examiner will test you

Your examiner will watch carefully to see that you use the OSM/PSL routine and select the correct lane in good time. You should

- plan ahead and choose the correct lane in good time
- use the OSM/PSL routine correctly
- position your vehicle sensibly, even if there are no road markings.

Faults to avoid - You shouldn't

- ride too close to the kerb or to the centre of the road
- change lanes at the last moment or without good reason
- hinder other road users by being badly positioned or being in the wrong lane
- cut across the path of other traffic in another lane at roundabouts.

You can't know what is around some corners. Make sure you take up the correct position and ride at a speed where you can stop in the distance that you can see to be clear

Pedestrian crossings

What the test requires

You should

- recognise the different types of pedestrian crossing
- show courtesy and consideration towards pedestrians
- stop safely when necessary.

At zebra crossings

You must slow down and stop if there is anyone on the crossing.

You should also

- slow down and be prepared to stop if there is anyone waiting to cross
- know how to give the correct arm signal, if necessary, before slowing down or stopping.

At pelican, puffin and toucan crossings

You must

- stop if the lights are red
- give way to any pedestrians on a pelican crossing when the amber lights are flashing
- give way to cyclists on a toucan crossing, as you would to pedestrians.

How your examiner will test you

Your examiner will watch carefully and take account of how you deal with pedestrian crossings.

You should be able to

- approach a pedestrian crossing at a controlled speed
- stop safely when necessary
- move off when it's safe, keeping a good lookout.

Faults to avoid - You shouldn't

- approach a crossing too fast
- ride over a crossing without stopping or showing awareness of waiting pedestrians
- block a crossing by stopping on it
- overtake within the zigzag white lines leading up to crossings
- wave pedestrians across
- take late or incorrect action on traffic light signals at controlled crossings.

Don't hurry pedestrians across a crossing by sounding your horn, revving your engine or edging forward.

Selecting a safe place to stop

What the test requires

When you make a normal stop you should be able to select a place where you won't obstruct the road or create a hazard. You should stop close to the edge of the road.

How your examiner will test you

Your examiner will take account of your use of the OSM/PSL routine and your judgement in selecting a safe place to stop.

You should know how and where to stop without causing inconvenience or danger to other road users.

Faults to avoid - You shouldn't

- stop without sufficient warning to other road users
- cause danger or inconvenience to other road users when you stop.

Your examiner will ask you to stop in a convenient place. You will have to choose where to stop and pull up close to the edge of the road

Awareness and anticipation

What the test requires

You should be aware of other road users at all times. You should

- judge what other road users are likely to do
- predict how their actions will affect you
- react safely and in good time.

You should show awareness of, and consideration for, all other road users. Anticipation of possible danger and concern for safety should also be shown.

How your examiner will test you

Pedestrians - Give way to pedestrians when turning from one road to another.

Take particular care with the very young, the disabled and the elderly. They may misjudge your speed or may not be aware of you.

Cyclists - Take special care

- when crossing bus or cycle lanes
- with cyclists passing on your left
- with child cyclists.

Animals can be unpredictable. Drop your speed and be prepared to stop

Animals - Take special care around animals. Give horse riders and other animal handlers as much room as you can. Watch young, possibly inexperienced, riders closely for signs of any difficulty with their mounts. Plan your approach carefully.

Faults to avoid - You shouldn't

- react suddenly to road or traffic conditions
- show irritation with other road users
- sound the horn aggressively
- rev your engine or edge forward when waiting for pedestrians to cross a road.

section **five**
RETESTING

This section covers

- New Drivers Act
- The extended test

New Drivers Act

Special rules apply for the first two years after the date of passing your first practical test if you held nothing but a provisional licence before passing your test.

How you may be affected

Your licence will be revoked if the number of penalty points on your licence reaches six or more as a result of offences you commit before the two years are over. This includes offences you committed before passing your test.

You must then apply for a provisional licence and complete CBT before riding on the road.

You may ride only as a learner until you pass the theory and practical test again.

This applies even if you pay by fixed penalty.

The New Drivers Act was brought in to help keep the roads safer for all road users. Riders who obey the law will not be affected

The extended test

Tough penalties exist for anyone convicted of dangerous driving or riding offences.

Courts must impose an extended test on anyone convicted of dangerous driving or riding offences.

Courts can also

- impose an extended driving or riding test on anyone convicted of other offences involving obligatory disqualification
- order a normal-length test for other endorsable offences before the disqualified driver or rider can recover a full licence.

The extended test is assessed to the same standard as the learner test but lasts for about 70 minutes. This makes it more demanding due to the longer time devoted to normal riding

Applying for a retest

A rider subject to a retest can apply for a provisional licence at the end of the disqualification period. CBT must be completed before riding on the road.

The normal rules for provisional licence-holders apply

- L plates (or, if you wish, D plates in Wales) must be displayed to the front and rear of the machine
- solo motorcycles must not exceed 125 cc and 11 kW power output (unless riding under the Direct Access Scheme)
- riding on motorways isn't allowed
- pillion passengers may not be carried.

You can book an extended test in the same way as a normal test (see section three).

The theory test

You will have to pass the theory test before an application for the practical test can be made.

Details of the theory test can be found in section three.

Longer and more demanding

The extended test takes about 70 minutes and covers a wide variety of roads, usually including dual carriageways. This test is more demanding, so make sure that you are ready.

You are advised to take suitable instruction from an approved motorcycle trainer.

Higher fees

The higher fee reflects the longer duration of the test.

How your examiner will test you

Your test will include all the exercises included in the normal test. Your examiner will watch you and take account of

- your ability to concentrate for the duration of the test
- your attitude to other road users.

At the start of the test you'll have to read and sign a declaration. You are signing to confirm your machine is suitably insured and also to confirm your UK residency status

section **six**

FURTHER INFORMATION

This section covers
- If you pass
- If you don't pass
- Recommended syllabus
- Service standards

If you pass

Well done! You will have shown that you can ride safely.

Your examiner will give you a copy of the Driving Test Report which will show any riding faults which have been marked during the test and some notes to explain this report.

Your examiner will then ask for your provisional licence so that an upgraded licence can automatically be sent to you through the post. They will take your provisional licence and, once the details have been taken, will shred it. You will be given a pass certificate (DSA10) as proof of success, until you receive your new licence.

If you don't want to surrender your licence you don't have to, and there will be certain circumstances when this isn't possible, if for example you have changed your name.

In these cases you'll have to send your provisional licence together with your pass certificate and the appropriate fee to DVLA, and they'll send you your full licence. You have to do this within two years or you'll have to take your test again.

Look at the test report carefully and discuss it with your instructor. It includes notes to help you understand how the examiner marks the form.

You may then find it helpful to refer to the relevant sections in this book to help you overcome those weaknesses noted during your test.

Remember, under the New Drivers Act your licence could be revoked if you receive six or more penalty points within two years of passing your first test.

Developing your riding standards

You should aim to raise your standard of riding with additional instruction and experience.

Learning doesn't stop after you remove your L plates. Ask your instructor about further training including motorway riding

If you don't pass

Your riding isn't up to the standard required. You made mistakes which could have caused danger on the road.

Your examiner will help you by

- giving you a driving test report form. This will show all the faults marked during the test
- explaining briefly why you haven't passed.

Listen to your examiner carefully. They will be able to help you by pointing out the aspects of your riding which you need to improve.

Study the driving test report. It will include notes to help you understand how the examiner marks the form. You may then find it helpful to refer to the relevant sections in this book.

Show your copy of the report to your instructor who will advise and help you to correct the faults. Listen to their advice carefully and get as much practice as you can.

Right of appeal

You will obviously be disappointed if you don't pass your motorcycle test. Although your examiner's decision can't be changed, if you think your test wasn't carried out according to the regulations, you have the right to appeal.

If you live in England and Wales you have six months after the issue of the Statement of Failure in which to appeal (Magistrates' Courts Act 1952 Ch. 55 part VII, Sect. 104).

If you live in Scotland you have 21 days in which to appeal (Sheriff Court, Scotland Act of Sederunt (Statutory Appeals) 1981).

Recommended syllabus

Riding is a life skill. It will take you many years to acquire the skills set out here to a high standard. This syllabus lists the skills in which you must achieve basic competence. You must also have

- a thorough knowledge of *The Highway Code* and motoring laws
- understanding of your responsibilities as a rider.

This means that you must have real concern, not just for your own safety but for the safety of all road users, including pedestrians.

Legal requirements

To learn to ride on the road you must

1 be aged at least 16 years if you wish to ride a moped, or 17 years if you wish to ride a motorcycle.

2 be able to read in good daylight (with glasses or contact lenses, if you wear them) a vehicle number plate with letters 79.4 mm (3.1 inches) high at a minimum distance of 20.5 metres (about 67 feet).

Number plates in the format (XX50XXX) have a narrower font and should be read from a distance of 20 metres (66 feet).

3 be medically fit to hold a licence.

4 hold a provisional driving licence, or provisional riding entitlement on a full licence for another category.

5 comply with the requirements of a provisional licence

- hold a valid Compulsory Basic Training (CBT) certificate
- display L plates (or, if you wish, D plates in Wales) to the front and rear of the machine
- pillion passengers must not be carried
- riding on motorways isn't allowed
- solo motorcycles must not exceed 125 cc or 11 kW power output unless learning under the Direct Access Scheme (only open to those over 21 years old), where there are no restrictions to either size or power output.

6 ensure that the machine being ridden

- is legally roadworthy
- has a current test certificate if it's over the prescribed age
- displays a valid tax disc
- is covered by appropriate insurance.

7 be aware of the legal requirements to notify medical conditions which could affect safe riding. If a machine has been adapted for a disability, ensure that all the adaptations are suitable to control the machine safely.

8 wear a safety helmet when riding a motorcycle on road (members of the Sikh religion who wear a turban are exempt).

9 know the rules on the issue, presentation or display of driving licences, insurance certificates and tax discs.

Rider safety

You must know

1 the safety aspects relating to helmets and how to adjust a helmet correctly.

2 the safety factors in wearing suitable clothing and using goggles and visors.

Machine controls, equipment and components

You must

1 understand the function of the

- throttle
- clutch
- gears
- front and rear brakes
- steering

and be able to adjust (where applicable) and use these competently.

2 know the function of all other controls and switches and use them competently.

3 understand the meaning of the gauges and other displays on the instrument panel.

4 know the legal requirements for the machine.

5 be able to carry out routine safety checks such as

- the brakes for correct operation and adjustment
- the steering head for wear and adjustment
- oil and coolant levels
- tyre pressures
- chain tension and condition
- condition of control cables
- suspension
- wheels and tightness of nuts and bolts

and identify defects, especially with the

- steering
- brakes
- tyres
- lights
- reflectors
- direction indicators
- horn
- rear view mirrors
- speedometer
- exhaust system
- chain.

6 understand the effect that carrying a load or a pillion passenger will have on the handling of your machine.

Road user behaviour

You must

1 know the most common causes of accidents.

2 know which road users are most at risk and how to reduce that risk.

3 know the rules, risks and effects of drinking and riding.

4 know the effect of fatigue, illness and drugs on riding performance.

5 be aware of any age-related problems among other road users, especially among children, teenagers and the elderly.

6 be alert and able to anticipate the likely actions of other road users, and be able to take appropriate precautions.

7 be aware that courtesy and consideration towards other road users are essential for safe riding.

Machine characteristics

You must

1 know the important principles concerning braking distances and road holding under various road and weather conditions.

2 know the handling characteristics of other vehicles with regard to stability, speed, braking and manoeuvrability.

3 know that some vehicles are less easily seen than others.

4 be able to assess the risks caused by the characteristics of other vehicles and suggest precautions that can be taken, for example

- large commercial vehicles pulling to the right before turning left
- blind spots for some commercial vehicle drivers
- bicycles and other motorcyclists being buffeted by strong winds.

Road and weather conditions

You must

1 know the particular hazards in both daylight and darkness, and on different types of road, for example

- on single carriageways, including country lanes
- on three-lane roads
- on dual carriageways and motorways.

2 gain riding experience on urban and higher-speed roads (but not on motorways) in both daylight and darkness.

3 know which road surfaces provide the better or poorer grip when braking.

4 know the hazards caused by bad weather, for example

- rain
- fog
- snow
- ice
- strong winds.

5 be able to assess the risks caused by road and traffic conditions, be aware of how the conditions may cause others to drive or ride unsafely, and be able to take appropriate precautions.

Traffic signs, rules and regulations

You must have a sound knowledge of the meaning of traffic signs and road markings, for example

- speed limits
- parking restrictions
- zebra and pelican crossings.

Machine control and road procedure

You must have the knowledge and skills to carry out the following tasks safely and competently, practising the proper use of mirrors, observation and signals

1 take necessary precautions before mounting or dismounting the machine.

2 before starting the engine, carry out safety checks on

- controls
- mirrors.

Also check that the gear selector is in neutral.

3 start the engine and move off

- straight ahead and at an angle
- on the level, uphill and downhill.

4 select the correct road position for normal riding.

5 use proper observation in all traffic conditions.

6 be able to carry out additional safety checks for two-wheeled vehicles, for example by

- using the mirrors
- looking over the shoulder
- including the 'lifesaver' look.

7 be able to use the front and rear brakes correctly.

8 know how to lean while turning.

9 ride at a speed suitable for road and traffic conditions.

10 react promptly to all risks.

11 change traffic lanes.

12 pass stationary vehicles.

13 meet, overtake and cross the path of other vehicles.

14 turn right and left at junctions, including crossroads and roundabouts.

15 ride ahead at crossroads and roundabouts.

16 keep a safe separation distance when following other traffic.

17 act correctly at pedestrian crossings.

18 show proper regard for the safety of other road users, with particular care towards the most vulnerable.

19 ride on both urban and rural roads and, where possible, dual carriageways - keeping up with the flow of traffic where it's safe and proper to do so.

20 comply with traffic regulations and traffic signals given by the police, traffic officers, traffic wardens and other road users.

21 stop the machine safely, normally and in an emergency, without locking the wheels.

22 be able to make a U-turn safely.

23 be able to keep the machine balanced at all speeds.

24 be able to wheel the machine, without the aid of the engine, by walking alongside it.

25 be able to park and remove the machine from its stand.

26 cross all types of railway level crossing.

Additional knowledge

You must know

1 the importance of correct tyre pressures.

2 the action needed to avoid and correct skids.

3 how to ride through floods and flooded areas.

4 what to do if you are involved in an accident or breakdown, including the special arrangements for accidents or breakdowns on a motorway.

5 basic first aid for use on the road as set out in *The Highway Code*.

6 how to deter motorcycle thieves.

Motorway riding

You must gain a sound knowledge of the special rules, regulations and riding techniques for motorway riding before taking your riding test.

After passing your test, lessons are recommended with a motorcycle instructor before riding unsupervised on motorways.

Service standards

We judge our performance against the following standards (printed in our Business Plan) which we review each year

- 90% of customers will be satisfied with the overall level of service received
- 95% of calls to booking offices will make contact with our automated call-handling system without receiving an engaged tone
- after a call has gone through our automated call-handling system, we will answer 90% of all incoming calls to booking offices in no more than 20 seconds
- the national average waiting time for practical motorcycle tests will be no longer than four weeks
- we will keep 98% of appointments that are in place three days before the test appointment
- we will answer 97% of all letters and e-mails within 10 working days
- we will pay 95% of all refunds within 15 days of a receiving valid claim
- our online booking service will be available 99% of the time over 24 hours, seven days a week.

Complaints guide

We aim to give our customers the best possible service. Please tell us when

- we ve done well
- you aren't satisfied.

Your comments can help us to improve the service we offer.

For information about DSA service standards, contact DSA Test Enquiries and Booking Centre (see p3).

If you have any questions about how your test was conducted, please contact the local Supervising Examiner, whose address is displayed at your local driving test centre.

If you are dissatisfied with the reply or you wish to comment on other matters, you can write to DSA (see p3).

Finally, you can write to

The Chief Executive
Driving Standards Agency
Stanley House
56 Talbot Street
Nottingham NG1 5GU

None of this removes your right to take your complaint to

- your Member of Parliament, who may decide to raise your case personally with the DSA Chief Executive, the Minister, or the Parliamentary Commissioner for Administration (the Ombudsman), (see p3)
- a magistrates' court (in Scotland, to the Sheriff of your area) if you believe that your test wasn't carried out according to the regulations.

Before doing this, you should seek legal advice.

Refunding fees and expenses

DSA always aims to keep test appointments, but occasionally we have to cancel a test at short notice. We will refund the test fee, or give you your next test free, in the following circumstances

- if we cancel your test
- if you cancel a test and give us at least three working days' notice
- if you keep the test appointment but the test doesn't take place or isn't finished, for a reason that isn't your fault or the fault of the vehicle you are using.

We will also compensate you for the money you lost if we cancelled your test at short notice (unless it was for bad weather).

For example, we will pay

- the cost of hiring a vehicle for the test, including reasonable travelling time to and from the test centre
- any pay or earnings you lost, after tax and so on (usually for half a day).

We *won't* pay the cost of lessons which you arrange linked to a particular test appointment, or extra training you decide to take while waiting for a rescheduled test.

How to apply - Please write to the DSA Enquiries and Booking Centre and send a receipt showing hire charges, or an employer's letter which shows what earnings you lost. If possible, please use the standard form (available from every driving test centre or booking office) to make your claim.

These arrangements don't affect your legal rights.

The Official DSA Guide to Riding – the essential skills

This official DSA guide will help you acquire and maintain the skills necessary to keep you safe on the road.

Includes best riding practice, guidance and technique for learners, experienced riders and instructors – including defensive riding, all-weather riding techniques and basic maintenance.

ISBN 9780115526442

£12.99

Know Your Traffic Signs
Department for Transport

NEW EDITION JULY 2007

A new fully updated guide to traffic signs. This handy reference title illustrates and explains the vast majority of traffic signs that a road user is likely to encounter.

A thorough knowledge of all traffic signs is essential for all road users, not just new riders, making this the ideal companion to ensure your knowledge is up-to-date. Although The Official Highway Code contains most of the commonly used road signs which are prescribed by the Traffic Signs Regulations, it does not give a comprehensive explanation of our signing system. This is therefore a perfect complimentary title to The Official Highway Code.

ISBN 9780115528552

£4.99

The Official DSA Theory Test for Motorcyclists CD-ROM

Take your theory test with confidence, by preparing with this expert software guide valid for tests taken from 3rd September 2007.

Key features:

- Test yourself on every theory test question you could be asked in 2007/08
- The closest experience to the real multiple choice part of the theory test
- Analyses your test performance to identify which topics need more revision
- Sit customised tests, so you can practise specific topics more thoroughly.

ISBN 9780115528422

£12.99

Competition Rules

1   Only one entry accepted per purchase.

2   All entries must be on official entry forms. No photocopies will be accepted.

3   Entries must be received by 8 September 2008.

4   The competition will run from 23 July 2007 to 8 September 2008 and one prize shall be awarded. All entries must be received by 8 September 2008. No responsibility can be taken by the Promoter for lost, late, misdirected or stolen entries.

5   The prize will be a set of genuine Suzuki leathers or protective clothing, gloves, helmet and accessories to be selected by Suzuki at a value of about £1000 at time of going to press in its absolute discretion. Colour is subject to availability. The size of bike gear will be based on measurements supplied by the winner and accessories will be based on the type of bike to be used by the winner, upon request by Suzuki, failing which Suzuki shall be entitled to select reasonable sizes and accessories for the winner. There will be no cash alternatives.

6   Only entrants over the age of 16 and resident in the UK are eligible.

7   The winning entry will be decided on 10 September 2008 from all correct entries received by the closing date. The winner will be notified by 24 September 2008. Only the winner will be contacted personally.

8   The winner will be contacted via the email address or telephone number they provide. The Promoter will not be held responsible if the winner cannot be contacted by the means they gave.

9   The winner's name will be published on the Promoter's website at www.tso.co.uk.

10 The prize will be made available within six weeks of the closing date.

11 By accepting any Prize, entrants consent to the use for promotional and other purposes (without further payment and except as prohibited by law) of their name, address, likeness and Prize information. The winner may be required to participate in the Promoter's reasonable marketing and promotional activities. By entering into this competition you consent to participate in the Promoter's reasonable marketing and promotional activities. The winning entrant agrees that all rights including copyright in all works created by the entrant as part of the competition entry shall be owned by the Promoter absolutely without the need for further payment being made to the entrant. Such entrant further agrees to waive unconditionally and irrevocably all moral rights pursuant to the Copyright, Designs and Patents Act of 1988 and under any similar law in force from time to time anywhere in the world in respect of all such works.

12 The Promoter reserves the right to cancel this competition at any stage, if deemed necessary in its opinion, and if circumstances arise outside of its control.

13 Entrants will be deemed to have accepted these rules and to agree to be bound by them when entering this competition.

14 This competition is not open to employees or contractors of the Promoter or the Driving Standards Agency or any person directly involved in the organisation or running of the competition, or their direct family members. The judge's decision is final in every situation including any not covered above and no correspondence will be entered into.

15 The Promoter is The Stationery Office Limited, St Crispins, Duke Street, Norwich, NR3 1PD (the publishers of The Official DSA Learner Range).

What type of moped/ motorcycle is it?

....

Do you plan to buy a moped/ motorcycle when you pass?
Yes ☐ No ☐

If Yes, will the moped/ motorcycle be...
New ☐ Second-hand ☐

What type of moped/ motorcycle are you looking to own?

....

For what purposes do you propose to use your moped/ motorcycle?
Leisure ☐ Commuting ☐ For your work ☐ On-road ☐ Off-road ☐
Touring/ Holidays ☐ Sports/ Racing/ Track days ☐ Attending bike events ☐

Which publications do you read?

....

Name of shop or website that you bought this product from?

....

How would you improve this, or any other DSA product?

....

....

Name ....

Address ....

.... Date of birth ....

Daytime telephone number ....

Mobile telephone number ....

I have read, accept and agree to be bound by the Competition Rules

Signature .... Date ....

If you would like us to send you email updates on your specific area (s) of interest register at www.tsoshop.co.uk/signup.

* Terms and conditions apply

Competition Entry Form

To enter, simply answer the questions and tell us in 25 words or less how learning to ride will make a difference to your life. The winner will be the entrant who answers the first 3 questions below correctly and writes the most apt and original 25 word essay, as decided by the judges.

1. **You are following a vehicle on a wet road. You should leave a time gap of at least how many seconds?**

   ....

2. **What is the legal minimum depth of tread for motorcycle tyres in millimetres?**

   ....

3. **Why should you check over your shoulder before turning right into a side road?**

   ....

   ....

Tie Breaker: Learning to ride will change my life.... (complete in 25 words or less)

....

....

....

....

When are you planning/ hoping to take your theory test?
Within a fortnight ☐ Within a month ☐ In 1-3 months ☐ In 3-6 months ☐
In 6-12 months ☐ In 12+ months ☐

When are you planning/ hoping to take your practical test?
Within a fortnight ☐ Within a month ☐ In 1-3 months ☐ In 3-6 months ☐
In 6-12 months ☐ 12+ months ☐

Do you already own a moped/ motorcycle?
Yes ☐ No ☐

If Yes, is the moped/ motorcycle...
New ☐ Second-hand ☐

The **OFFICIAL DSA GUIDE** to
LEARNING
TO RIDE

WIN OFFICIAL
SUZUKI GEAR*

The publisher of the Official DSA Learner Range, TSO, is offering you the chance to win new Suzuki clothing or accessories.

Other Official DSA Publications

The Official Highway Code

Essential reading for all road-users, the only official Highway Code in the market contains the very latest rules of the road. Many of these rules are legal requirements and must be adhered to, in order to avoid penalty – fines, penalty points, disqualification or even prison.

Make sure you're aware of the most up-to-date rules of the road.

The Official Highway Code – for life, not just for learners.

ISBN 9780115526985 £1.99

The Official DSA Guide to Hazard Perception DVD

Hazard perception is a vital skill and a key part of today's driving tests. This interactive DVD from the Driving Standards Agency, will help you stay safe on the roads.

Includes the official DSA video clips and tests your responses to hazards in real time.

ISBN 9780115524943 £15.99